Taming the BIG PHARMA MONSTER

by Speaking Truth to Power

Hedley Rees

Published by
Filament Publishing Ltd.
16 Croydon Road, Beddington
Croydon, Surrey, CR0 4PA, United Kingdom
www.filamentpublishing.com
Telephone: +44 (0)208 688 2598

© 2019 Hedley Rees

ISBN 978-1-912635-91-7
Printed by 4edge Ltd

The right of Hedley Rees to be recognised as the author of this work has been asserted by him in accordance with the Designs and Copyright Act 1988.

This book may not be copied in any way without the prior written permission of the publishers.

DEDICATION

For Pedro Hernandez
in memoriam

True friend of modernisation
in the medicines industry.

Evangelist and pioneer of Quality by Design
(QbD) and Process Analytical Technology
(PAT).

Man of integrity and passion for
doing the right thing. Educator, learner
and developer of people.

Sadly no longer with us in body,
but his spirit lives on.

Thank you for your
groundbreaking work, Pedro.

CONTENTS

PREFACE 7
1. DISRUPTING BIG PHARMA? DO ME A FAVOUR 13
2. HOUSTON, WE'VE HAD A PROBLEM 19
3. RETURN TO A PCs YOUTH 25
4. 'FEMME FATALE' SCIENCE TURNS PC HEADS 31
5. PCs JETTISON THEIR ASSETS 35
6. PANIC AND CONFUSION REIGN IN THE INDUSTRY 43
7. WHAT ARE THE HARSH REALITIES FOR PCs? 65
8. IT'S THE SYSTEM WOT DONE IT, YOUR HONOUR 93
9. THE PEOPLE-PURPOSE (PPS) SYSTEM STEPS IN TO HELP ... 113
10. BROKE'S NO FUN - TIME TO APPLY THE FIX 123

APPENDICES

1. EDUCATION PROGRAMME AND WORKSHOP 137
2. MEDICINES FOR THE 21ST CENTURY - FACILITATION PANEL ... 141

REFERENCES 147

PREFACE

I almost didn't write this book. My maiden and two subsequent attempts, despite receiving great reviews, were disappointing in terms of sales. I had been certain the world was hungry to hear the messages within, not just to inform and educate on my speciality subject – strategic management of the supply chain – but also to help catalyse change for the better in the medicines (pharmaceutical) industry, with tongue-in-cheek accounts of what's been going on, and wrong.

As I think back, the important messages were about as popular as the Conservative Club in Moscow to a world believing there was no better, more patient-centred way.

Undeterred, I have continued to preach the messages at conferences, in professional journals, and through webcasts and podcasts. The presentation I give is purposefully provocative. I've resorted to giving the drug development and commercialisation process a funny name - find it, file it, flog it - and semi-ridiculing the notion of scientists discovering blockbuster drugs in the dead of night, surrounded by test tubes, Bunsen burners and other apparatus involved in deep chemistry.

The audiences are mainly polite. People tend not to challenge me on what I say, although there must be a lot of skepticism underneath. Only once have I been taken to task, at a conference, by an industry leader who appeared greatly irritated by such frank expression of opinion that was clearly counter to his own. It took me by surprise at the time.

I have recently been toying with the idea of writing something even more direct and explicit than my previous attempts, accessible to an informed patient, industry professionals and other key stakeholders. Something has been stopping me, though. It's one thing shouting in the dark when people aren't listening, but if they do listen and take it all in, that would place a whole new burden of responsibility on me to follow through with it.

For reassurance, I recently returned to my copy of *The War of Art* by Steven Pressfield. His view is that creativity is blood, sweat, and tears, and a fight against the fear of creating something at which others will pick, often deeply. It requires a steely determination to keep resisting the knot in your stomach telling you to stop and pursue more tranquil endeavours, to turn up at your desk every morning to write the next instalment.

That wasn't the only source of reassurance.

Firstly, there was Mrs Madeleine Moon, MP for Bridgend. I sent her a copy of a paper I had previously submitted to a House of Lords inquiry into life sciences in the UK. There was little if any response from the enquiry committee, so I emailed Mrs. Moon, as my constituency MP, to ask why this might have been the case. I also sent her a copy of the paper. She then asked to meet me and, since then, she has been fighting our corner at every opportunity despite her gruelling schedules.

The following is Mrs Moon's account

'I receive many emails each week asking me to support a wide variety of causes ranging from the armed forces to medical and environmental campaigns, so when Mr. Rees wrote to me asking about a paper he had submitted to the UK House of Lords Committee Inquiry into Life Sciences and Industrial Strategy, I read it and was intrigued by its contents. It seemed to address, head-on, issues of medicines affordability, accessibility, R&D productivity and speed to market. It also appeared to offer up solutions to a politician that seemed eminently sensible.

'As one of my constituents, I have duly taken his corner and have made the Health and Social Care Committees of UK and Welsh

Preface

Governments aware of the initiative this book is a companion to. I have also sent details to several All-Party Parliamentary Groups (APPGs) with an interest in the topic area.

'In the press release announcing the inception of this initiative, I was pleased to comment as follows:

'"It is time that we explored ways of improving accessibility and reducing the amount of time it takes to bring new medicines to market. It will be interesting to see whether the specialists can teach the pharmaceutical industry new approaches to tackle these challenges."'

So we wait and see what they come up with. Judging by the weight of skill and experience on the facilitation panel, and the impressive number of patient representatives and healthcare professionals attending, we may be in for a very pleasant treat!

Next inspiration and reinforcement comes from Mark Duman.

I describe Mark to people as a force of nature, mainly because he is. Mark is to networking what Muhammad Ali was to boxing: he floats like a butterfly and stings like a bee – in metaphorical terms of course.

We met in a pub in Paddington, home of every Welshman's train trip over the border into England, on the road to Twikkers. It was early in 2016. He had scribbled all over the copy of the *FIFIFI* book I'd sent him for review. He was enthusiastic about what he had read, and ever since has used his 'bee sting' to get me a hearing with senior UK folk in the medicines industry and politics.

Results have been predictable, if I'm honest. I expect the brush-off now in the knowledge that those within an established system are rarely disposed towards changing it. Expecting it and accepting it is another matter, however. Being even more honest, I hate it; but the frogs are there to be kissed and someone has to do it.

I just wish it wasn't me. Most of what you read in this book, though, luckily, is about the prince and princesses who did the switch along the way, or those who were never a frog in the first place.

Indirectly though, this led me to the breakthrough I'm describing today. At Mark's suggestion, I penned the paper that Mrs. Moon was able to read, digest and get behind.

Next on the list is an organisation, not a person. It is LinkedIn (LI). I didn't include Jeff Weiner in the section on industry giants so as not to overload readers, but he is squarely in there. You will learn what qualities it needs to qualify later, but suffice to say that the LI product offering is phenomenal value for money – if charging zilch, zippo, and diddly-squat is any measure of value.

For zero smackeroonies, you get to put your full profile out there, available to the world of business and enterprise, and you can view others minded to do the same thing. For those you take a shine to, the opportunity is there to invite them to connect with you. It might take a politely worded note, drawing attention to your shared interests and plans, but that is more than compensated by the joy of connection with a like-minded soul.

There is no pressure to do any more than that. When the time is ripe, opportunities may arise to speak more on a topic, but no pressure. Over time, as you make more connections and become increasingly visible, others invite you, rather than just vice versa. You start to build a powerful network that can work for you, and you for it.

I should stop here now for the sake of brevity, but I'm only scratching the surface of what you get for free. Guilty conscience has led me to take up the LI premier service of late, but I could still manage well without it.

Next source of inspiration are the facilitation panel members, listed in the appendix. They don't know they are an inspiration, of course - why would they? All they have agreed to is to join a list, having no idea what arrangements were in place to make the initiative happen, and if it were to happen, what that participation would involve. But for them, being on a public list supporting an event like this is not to be taken lightly. This list has been shared far and wide and not one has asked for their names to be removed. Hopefully, they will turn up on the day!

Now we turn to Janet Woodcock MD. The wiley editor for *Pharmaceutical Sciences*, Jonathan Rose, who commissioned my first book, suggested I seek permission to add Dr. Woodcock's name as a contributor, given I had used some of her pronouncements taken from the FDA website. I wasn't quite sure how I would get to such a prominent person so took a stab at finding her on the FDA website - and there she was, email address staring up at me.

I wasn't getting excited yet because I still had to ask the question, which I did. The following day, I had her permission.

As the years have gone by, Dr. Woodcock has never failed to respond to my occasional emails requesting various snippets of information. Even so, it was not without trepidation that I made the request for her to record the keynote address. Before I knew it, my email was forwarded to the FDA digital communications team, headed by Paul Buckman, and the recording was slotted into the schedule.

The penultimate inspiration is Chris Day and his team at Filament Publishing. They have been a delight to work with and have restored my faith in the publishing industry - no budding author needs to surrender their manuscript to predatory publishers while Filament is around.

As a blatant act of raging self-interest, special mention is made of Liz Sheppard-Jones who is editing this work and keeping me on the straight and narrow.

Taming the Big Pharma Monster

The final inspiration is the venue for our conference, and its location. Nestled in the once infamous dock area in Cardiff Bay, transformed by the city into a stunning waterside cultural and entertainment attraction, lies Techniquest. I will leave Lesley Kirkpatrick, CEO, to welcome you to it:

'Welcome to Techniquest, Cardiff's leading science discovery centre and home to innovative interactive science experiences in Wales.

'At Techniquest, it's our mission to create a STEM-literate society (Science, Technology, Engineering and Mathematics) across Wales by making these essential foundational skills accessible to all. Our nation is home to a rich STEM heritage coupled with smart innovation, and we've pledged to make STEM-related learning exciting for everyone who comes through our doors, as well as inspire the future STEM workforce across Wales.

'While we are a beloved local institution, many people are unaware that we are an educational charity and that we deliver nurturing and inspirational educational programmes to over 73,000 school pupils across Wales. Over the next year, we'll be marching forward with our transformational project, 'The Science Capital'. This project encompasses a radical transformation of our current building, with an extension set to double our footprint. We hope you'll join us on our journey and come back to visit when we reveal our brand-new interactive science hub in summer 2020.

'We're thrilled to be involved with PharmaFlow's vital exploration into modern medicine, and we're incredibly proud to be setting the stage for the 'Medicines for the 21st Century' conference. With a naturally curious eye and passion for the future of STEM-related activities, we're looking forward to hearing from the inspiring panel of experts as they explore the challenges, approaches and sustainability of the pharmaceutical industry.'

1: DISRUPTING THE PHARMA INDUSTRY? DO ME A FAVOUR...

PLEASE, SUSPEND JUDGEMENT UNTIL YOU'VE HEARD OUR CASE

There aren't too many people willing to countenance the potential disruption of the pharma (from here on referred to as 'medicines') industry. In fact, there is probably no-one who would give houseroom to the notion – but it is possible. If this book achieves nothing other than convincing you of that, then we have a result on our hands.

So, give your brain a quick swill, wash out your pre-conceived ideas, and sit back for a fascinating few hours.

A UNIQUE INITIATIVE, NOT A MOMENT TOO SOON

This book is pre-reading for a unique initiative aiming to transform the approach pharmaceutical companies, (from here on referred to as PCs), take to developing and commercialising medicines – root, branch, twig and leaf.

Our underpinning message is that serendipity is no friend when it comes to developing new products for end-user markets. The notion that medicines are discovered by accident, during scientific experimentation, is complete nonsense.

The truth is that to bring a medicine to market, there needs to be intense collaboration between many players, and this collaboration MUST be stage-managed from the start as a complete programme of inter-related activities. We shall prove that creating a medicine should be no different to developing a plane, car, aero-engine or silicon chip.

In proving that, our ambition then is to convince the world that there is not a moment to lose. The wheels of change must begin to turn with ever greater velocity as patients and Friends of Medicines Modernisation (FOMM) are empowered to take on the challenge.

PATIENTS AS INDUSTRY DISRUPTORS, AND THEIR FOMM ALLIES

For our work to appeal to the world of business, it must be founded on the good honest principles of commercial success. Accordingly, we refer to the much-vaunted topic of disruption, or more accurately, disruptive innovation, a term coined by a gentleman named Clayton M. Christenson.

Christenson uses Ford as an example of what is, and what isn't, disruptive innovation. He and his team point out that initially, the automobile itself was not disruptive; it was an expensive luxury item, not able to challenge the incumbent horse-drawn vehicles used for transportation. When Ford came along with his mass-producible product, however, it was only then that the seeds of disruption were sown and the rest is history.

The world of medicines is, today, the horse-drawn carriage. We will be introducing it to the Model-T Ford in these pages.

There are many with vested interests in maintaining the status quo in this industry. For change to take hold, we must search out and engage with those non-vested individuals, companies and organisations willing to take up the challenge ahead.

Chapter One

As it stands today, the only clearly and undeniably 'non-vested entity' is a patient with a disease, or 'indication', as the industry jargon would have it. 'A friend in need is a friend indeed,' as the saying goes. We are all patients at some point in our lives. This book is therefore for you, me, our friends and family — and society at large.

WHAT SHOULD YOU EXPECT TO FIND HERE?

In here we explore a new way to develop and produce prescription medicines. Not a new way to develop products, however. In fact, the ideas are not new at all. We merely recognise that development of medicines should be treated no differently to any other product bound for consumer markets. There is a tried and tested approach to bringing products successfully to market, defined by exemplary sectors such as semiconductors, automotive and aerospace.

This model has been adopted across numerous industry sectors, following the Japanese revolution beginning in the 1960s. Then we learned that a steely focus on the end-user, and their value-for-money proposition, could deliver remarkable business success. This is what we hope to prove to the medicines industry in the work that follows — but who is 'we'?

Firstly, there will be expert witnesses, those more knowledgeable than I on specialist topics. They have been handpicked for their unique perspective on the medicines industry of today, but also, crucially importantly, have their eyes firmly fixed on a different and better future for medicines developers.

Their views may not always mirror mine in every respect, but there is an important thread that binds us together: a crushing desire to be part of the solution for the medicines industry. Not *the* solution, because only the industry has control over that, but to contribute insights and expertise that can get things going and help keep them on track.

Secondly, the Morgan family taken from *Find It, File It, Flog It* - simple folk who took a wrong fork in the road, seduced by easy profits and a comfortable lifestyle, based on flogging therapeutic sausages to unsuspecting, protein-deficient vegetarians.

We will hear from the son of these Welsh hill farmers, David Morgan and his dad, John. David was confused and bemused after the family received advice from local bank manager (they had them in those days), Evan Bevan, 'a powerful man in the village'. Things went pear-shaped and the family appears to be paying the price now.

Then there's me aiming to make sense of where things are today, hoping to help sort out a path, along with others here present, for the future of medicines development. I should therefore say something about myself.

In December 2015, I self-published the book mentioned above: *Find It, File It, Flog It* (FIFIFI). It was prompted by years of frustration with the modus operandi of the medicines industry. Not frustration in the normal sense - being hacked off when things outside your control go wrong. No, this was a deep personal sense of responsibility to help make it right. It felt like I had seen a murder and no-one wanted to hear about it.

I'd had an education and early career background outside the industry as an industrial and production engineer. Both are callings charged with producing things and improving complex systems of people working together to meet purposeful ends, employing all manner of enabling physical assets and technologies in the process. In more recent years, these have become known as 'socio-Technical Systems', a topic we will drill down into later in the book under a new title of people-purpose systems (PPS).

During my days studying and travelling by train to and from university in Cardiff in the mid-1970s, I had always been taken

Chapter One

with the huge sign on the roof of a factory as we passed the town of Bridgend (South Wales): 'Miles Laboratories, the makers of Alka Selzer'. In 1980, as fate would have it, I joined them as an employee and entered the world of pharmaceutical production and supply.

The company had recently been acquired by Bayer AG, who many will know as a global player in the chemical and pharmaceutical industries. Coincidentally and unbeknownst to me, this was the dawning of the age of 'blockbuster' drugs (medicines), which I now realise is the reason for my deep and ever-growing frustration – the reason why I wrote FIFIFI.

That book sold only a handful of copies. No, I'm lying, it sold fewer than that. On reflection, it never had a chance because it was advocating radical change. Not tinkering at the edges, but massive re-alignment of the status quo. As Machiavelli warns us in his now well-worn quote from *The Prince*:

'There is nothing more difficult to take in hand, more perilous to conduct, or more uncertain in its success, than to take the lead in the introduction of a new order of things.'

SEPARATING FACT FROM FICTION

After reading this book, you will be able to separate fact from the various fictional accounts of what is going on in the industry. Pharmaceutical companies and their trade associations put forward their view of the world, as do various media outlets and professional communications agencies. The level of interest in the truth varies greatly, but one thing is certain: it is almost impossible to gain an objective view of the rights and wrongs of all that is going on. This book aims to correct that.

We will therefore be hard on facts and evidence. We will put blame aside to focus on a positive view of the future, although much of it will make you wonder how it ever got into this mess.

MORE THAN A GENERATION OF CHANGE IS REQUIRED

The final point to take from this book is the scale of the change required. You will learn here that the steady decline for pharmaceutical companies started around forty years ago. It will take at least that amount of time while systems of education catch up, executives acquire new skills and competencies, industry professionals respond to revised ways of working, and stakeholders club together in collaborative ways that have previously remained untapped. There is no quick fix on offer here.

It is now time to write all this up so let's get on with it.

2 : HOUSTON, WE'VE HAD A PROBLEM

ADDICTIVE GAMBLER IN DENIAL

There's no way to soften the blows in this chapter, as the evidence will be stark, substantial, and downright frightening at times. It is in reaction to that fright that we call on PCs to wake up to the errors of the past and opportunities of the future.

Addiction experts will tell us that the first step in any journey of reform and re-invention is to admit there's a problem, and that radical change is not only necessary – it is a matter of survival, a life or death opportunity.

At this point we take stock on behalf of the addict, perform a state of the nation review of the medicines industry, and define the scale of the task ahead.

Through the book, we will draw on wisdom wrapped up in songs, films and giants of the industrial world. The country music icon Kenny Rogers has his say here. Fans of Kenny will be familiar with the lyrics from his classic song *'The Gambler'*:

On a warm summer's eve
On a train bound for nowhere
I met up with the gambler
We were both too tired to sleep

So we took turns a-starin'
Out the window at the darkness
The boredom overtook us,
And he began to speak

Before listening to the man's words, please take a moment to consider that here we have, metaphorically, pharma company leadership and investors 'staring at the darkness', wondering which way to turn, and there's a ton of evidence lending weight to the predicament faced. We will be covering more on this topic soon, but for now, we can summarise one crucial aspect which has been dubbed 'Eroom's Law'.

It states: 'The number of new drugs approved per billion US dollars spent on R&D has halved roughly every nine years since 1950, falling around 80-fold in inflation-adjusted terms'.

Time to break out the whiskey and continue:...

He said, 'Son, I've made a life
Out of readin' people's faces,
Knowin' what the cards were
By the way they held their eyes

'So if you don't mind me sayin''
I can see you're out of aces,
For a taste of your whiskey
I'll give you some advice'

Pharma executives are indeed out of aces. In fact, it seems they are mightily short of Kings, Queens and Jacks too!

Let's now return to the story as the whiskey, metaphorically, changes hands:

So, I handed him my bottle
And he drank down my last swallow
Then he bummed a cigarette
And asked me for a light

And the night got deathly quiet
And his face lost all expression

Chapter Two

*He said, 'If you're gonna play the game, boy,
You gotta learn to play it right*

*'You've got to know when to hold 'em,
Know when to fold 'em,
Know when to walk away
And know when to run*

*You never count your money
When you're sittin' at the table,
There'll be time enough for countin'
When the dealin's done'*

There is a massive lesson here. Although poker is gambling, it is also a game of skill and ingenuity. It requires years of practice and application to eventually learn how to beat the odds.

Over the last 40+ years, the medicines industry has changed the game fundamentally, from its being akin to poker into a game of roulette fast approaching the Russian variety. It has taken to gambling on molecular compounds with a patent behind them in the hope they strike lucky. It has become a game of numbers. The impact has been nuclear.

WHAT IS THE EXTENT OF THE PROBLEM?

As we write this, prices of many prescription medicines have reached a point where payers in the healthcare system can't afford them. Only last year, I read an article recounting how Gilead Sciences Inc.'s drug 'Yescarta' had only been administered to five patients two months after launch in the US. The price tag for the treatment was $373,000. The waiting list amounted to over 200, but patients' insurance would not cover the cost. It's not hard to imagine how those patients must have felt.

This is not an isolated incident - in fact, it has become the norm. Just after reading about Yescarta, I read of Spark Therapeutics Inc.'s drug 'Luxturna' priced at $850,000 per treatment being judged vastly overpriced in the US by the Institute for Clinical and Economic Review.

Earlier, Novartis had launched 'Kymriah' in the US in August, 2017 with a $475,000 price tag.

'Glybera', the first gene therapy drug to be launched in Europe, was priced at $1M, and unsurprisingly, was withdrawn from the market having sold diddly-squat.

This year, 2019, media reports announced the launch of 'Zolgensma' (AveXis), a gene therapy for spinal muscular atrophy (SMA) which has been filed with the FDA and EMA and is set to gain approval in both regions in the first half of 2019. Novartis hit the headlines when it suggested its price could be around the $4m (€3.5m) mark. Yes, you read correctly.

Based on the above, we must ask: what company can survive in the long term when its customers cannot afford to buy its products? Or is the industry hoping that global healthcare budgets will win the lottery?

The above is merely a snapshot in time and aims to represent a picture anyone with a computer and access to an internet search engine could paint for themselves; some of you may have tried it already. If not, feel free to have a go.

TOP TEN PHARMAS MAKE NEARLY $500bn in 2017

If we focus on the top ten pharmaceutical companies, we get an idea of how much business is going on. Below is a chart showing the market capitalisation and annual revenues (2017) of the top ten companies in the industry:

Chapter Two

COMPANY	MARKET CAP ($BN)	ANNUAL REVENUE ($BN)
Johnson & Johnson (NYSE:JNJ)	375	76
Pfizer (NYSE:PFE)	220	52
Roche Holdings (OTCMKTS:RHHBY)	210	55
Novartis (NYSE:NVS)	203	49
AbbVie (NYSE:ABBV)	170	28
Merck (NYSE:MRK)	166	40
Sanofi (NYSE:SNY)	107	43
Bayer (OTCMKTS:BAYRY)	107	40
Gilead Sciences (NASDAQ:GILD)	106	25
GlaxoSmithKline (NYSE:GSK)	95	30
TOTAL	1,759	438

These are mighty handsome numbers for investors to behold. If we also consider that these are *only* the top ten, and that no single company holds a double-digit market share, then there is an ungodly amount of money going into the industry pot. So, what has been going on?

Time to find out…

3 : RETURN TO A PCs YOUTH

IT WASN'T ALWAYS LIKE THIS

It has recently struck me that the medicines industry for many people has always been the same as it is today. A trade journal reporter declaring that 'pharma has traditionally been business-to-business' confirmed this realisation. This is certainly not the case, and those of more mature years, such as myself, remember a different time. The reporter's comment made me wonder how this perception occurred and how widespread it was. If the misconception is common, then I should explain.

When today's PCs were in their infancies in the 1950s, things were very different.

GlaxoSmithKline (then Glaxo) started by making powdered milk for babies. Beecham's (now GlaxoSmithKline) was famous for its 'flu powders, Johnson & Johnson was famous for baby hair shampoo, and Novartis wasn't even a twinkle in its grandfather's eye. The blockbuster hadn't been invented, and Big Pharma companies generally had clear views of the customer constituencies they were serving.

All had an underpinning focus on the need to satisfy patients first. The words of George W. Merck, the founder of Merck & Co. provides evidence:

'We try never to forget that medicine is for the people. It is not for the profits. The profits follow, and if we have remembered that, they have never failed to appear. The better we have remembered it, the larger they have been!'

That was life before the blockbuster era.

NOW WHAT'S GOING ON IN THE WELSH HILLS?

David Morgan got up from the kitchen table to answer the knock at the farmhouse door. At the door was a strangely dressed man with a cloak around his shoulders. He explained that he was a prince consort from a far-off land. With a troubled look on his face, he explained that his people, who were vegetarian, were getting sick from a diet lacking in protein. The wise men had researched the issue and concluded that a diet including meat was the only treatment, and that Welsh pork sausages were the best. He asked if the Morgan farm would be interested in supplying them with prime sausages.

David introduced his father, John and mother, Morfydd.

The prince consort explained what was needed. Meat was new to them so they had to be sure it did not upset their delicate tummies. This meant feeding raw pork to their cows, also used to a vegetarian diet. The cows may not like the pork, but it would be a good sign if they could stomach it.

Then they would feed the sausages in skins to the young, healthy soldiers in the army. They would be the ones least likely to suffer any permanent damage from the experience.

Afterward, a small number of the ailing people would sample some sausages. If it seemed they were beginning to return to health, they would sample more. In the end, if their condition was improving, no tummies were upset, and the sausages were made to princely standards defined by royalty, then sausages could go on sale to those in need.

In return, the prince consort said, the queen, who was a principled lady, would ensure that only sausages from the Morgan farm could be sold to her subjects for the following ten years.

So, it began. The Morgan family hired extended family, friends, most of the village, and those farther afield to find the pigs, develop the sausages, send all the information to the prince consort's office, and do the thousand and one other things necessary to get these sausages approved and on the market. Below is how it all began:

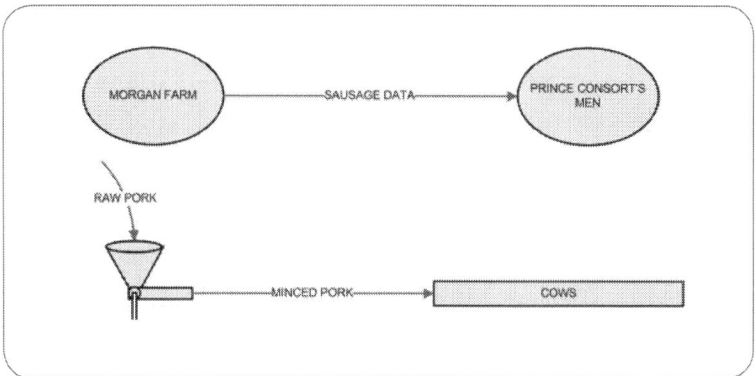

Testing the sausage meat in cows.

The raw pork was minced and sent to the far-off land to be fed to the cows. The data on how the pork was made, and its effect on the cows, were carefully collected and sent to the prince consort's wise men.

A thumbs up from the prince consort's men led onto the next stage shown below:

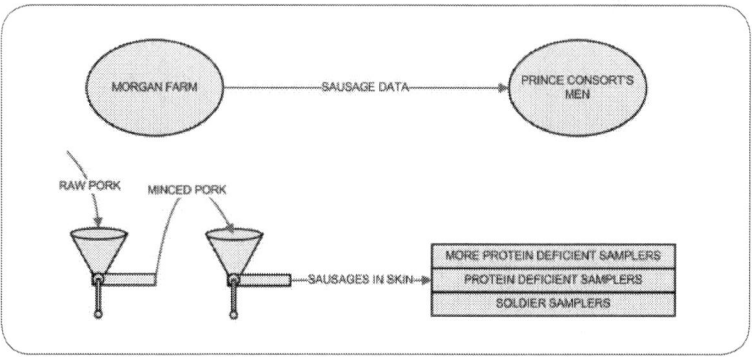

Testing sausages in skins on humans

The minced pork was filled into skins to be fed to samplers in the far-off land. A few of the soldiers suffered minor stomach upsets, but nothing too concerning. The subsequent sampling in the protein-deficient folk went well as several of them reported feeling better after a few weeks of downing the sausages.

A review of the data by the prince consort's men brought wonderful news: the sausages were succulent and approved for sale!

This is how it all meshed together:

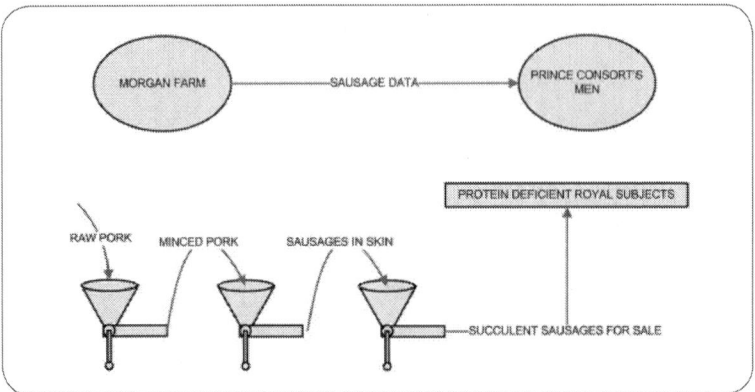

Selling succulent sausages to royal subjects

The project was a great success, and because the kingdom was very rich, the Morgans were paid handsomely for their work and did not have to worry about other families filling the sausage orders for a long time to come. They had more money coming in than they could ever have imagined, and they shared it with all involved.

REAL WORLD MEDICINES DEVELOPMENT

That was, of course, a fantasy to introduce the medicines development process in an easy to understand fashion.

Chapter Three

In the real world, compounds (new molecular entities or NMEs), selected as candidates for market must be proven safe to test in humans before clinical trials can begin. This is known as pre-clinical testing.

Pre-clinical testing involves proving that the medicine looks promising in a test-tube and is tolerated sufficiently well in animals to give a high level of assurance that it can be tested in healthy human volunteers without causing undue or irreversible harm. There is also an attempt to gather evidence that the medicine could be effective in treating the disease state under investigation. However, animals are much different from humans, so this is always sketchy at best and useless at worst. There is normally a requirement, though, for scientific rationale as to why the medicine should work in theory. That will have formed the basis of the patent award.

The sausage machine is a vital component of the whole system because it is physically what will be doing the magic work during clinical trials and when the medicine hits the market. The medicine to be fed to animals is purposely less pure than subsequent manufacture of the active ingredient for humans. This is known in the jargon as producing a 'dirty batch'. The logic is clear: as development proceeds, each subsequent batch becomes increasingly pure. The dirty batch is the 'worst case', and if the regulators are happy for a company to use it for initial testing, the process will only get easier over time.

If the pre-clinical phase gets approval, the company applies for and may receive a licence to run clinical trials in humans. This is known as a clinical trial application (CTA) in the European Union and an investigational new drug (IND) in the United States.

Phase I clinical testing is normally in healthy volunteers. All the data necessary are collected and the results assessed. Every clinical study must have a statistical 'end point(s)' that determines whether the study achieves what it has set out to prove. If it meets its end point(s), then it can progress to the next stage.

Phase II, sometimes divided into an A and a B, runs in patients with the condition under test.

Information is collected and, again, the company judges, through statistical analysis of the results, whether the study has met its end point(s). If it has, Phase III testing begins with a mission to gain approval from the regulators to market. If the regulators give approval, then it is hats in the air, yachts on order, and succulent sausages all round!

Surprising what sausage-making can tell you, eh?

The mathematicians among us may appreciate a little algebra to add meaning to the sausage analysis, by considering the equation below:

$S1 + S2 + S3 = ATS$

Where

$S1$ = Safe sausage (preclinical testing)

$S2$ = Sample sausage (clinical trials)

$S3$ = Succulent sausage (regulatory approval)

ATS = Approval To Sell

This pretty much describes the 20th century process for medicines development and approval that exists to this day. Any company developing medicines must follow along the same stages, no excuses or exclusions. Except... how they organise themselves to get through those stages is open to interpretation, as we soon discover.

4 : FEMME FATALE SCIENCE TURNS PC HEADS

THE CRUCIAL SEDUCTION UNEARTHED

In November 1976, Smith Kline & French (SK&F) launched 'Tagamet', a drug to combat stomach ulcers. It quickly took off and was dubbed the world's first 'blockbuster' drug ($\geq$ $1 bn annual sales). Glaxo launched a competitor product, 'Zantac', in 1981 and immediately targeted reportedly minor side-effects of Tagamet to pitch their case to doctors. By 1987, Zantac had become the world's biggest-selling prescription drug, outselling Tagamet 3:1 at one point.

This was the first example of clever targeting capturing competitor markets, and it stimulated phenomenal growth in the therapeutic area; the profits were immense for both companies, on sales of tens of billions of dollars. It was the beginning of a lucrative strategy for the industry.

Seduction turned to full-blown love following Glaxo's courtship display; the age of the blockbuster was upon us.

THIS WASN'T THE FIRST TIME SCIENCE TURNED PC HEADS

There is a further twist in this tale, relating to the well-known penicillin story. For those that need reminding, the mother of all antibiotics was discovered in 1928 by Alexander Fleming. On his return from holiday, he noticed that in one of his agar plates, bacteria had not grown. He obtained an extract from the mould in the plate, naming it 'penicillin'. The rest is history. Or is it...?

Actually, no. The *real* story goes like this.[1]

Fleming did not have the wherewithal to properly identify the mould strain or make it in any quantity. It took a team at Oxford University, headed by a gentleman named Howard Florey, to purify enough penicillin to run pre-clinical (1939) and clinical (1941) studies. They were a great success, but they didn't know how to make sufficient quantities to supply the market. In 1941, Florey and a fungal expert, Norman Heatley, visited the US to mull over the problem.

The scenario was put to a microbiologist named Andrew J. Moyer, an expert in moulds working at the USDA's Northern Regional Research Laboratory in Peoria, Illinois. He and his team came up with the idea 'to culture the penicillin in a mixture of corn steep liquor and lactose, thereby greatly increasing the yields and production rate.'

Moyer applied for a patent in May 1945, which was awarded three years later. He was inducted into the National Inventors Hall of Fame in 1987.

So why did the myth persist? An article in The Times reported the breakthrough in Oxford, but failed to mention Fleming or Florey. Fleming's boss wrote to the Times newspaper extolling his virtues and Fleming talked freely to the press at the time. Florey didn't say a dicky bird to the press. So the real account of it was never told.

WHAT WAS THE SEDUCTIVE MESSAGE?

'Medicine is discovered by accident—it's all a bit of a lottery, really. It needs clever scientists to discover active compounds by running lots and lots of experiments. Once the magic molecule pops up, we are home and dry.'

Here we have it, then. PCs had been softened up for seduction by a long-standing myth.

PCs TIE THE KNOT

PCs and their investors were mightily impressed by what Glaxo had achieved. Even the CEO of SK&F congratulated them on their win.

Armed with this apparently powerful strategic model, the large PCs (Big Pharma) resolved to beef up sales and marketing, awaiting molecules (also known as compounds) coming down the pipeline.

Discovery research grew like Topsy as great libraries of patented molecules were required to feed the hungry marketing machine.

Expert statisticians and medics were hired to help the marketers frame the messages to doctors. Regulatory affairs departments were expanded to be sure of keeping on the right side of the regulators.

So the scene was set. Sales and marketing, with their supporting cast, were poised ready for the next blockbuster molecule to come down the pipeline. Discovery research was out there, plotting theories on why a molecule would work, modelling and patenting them in great quantities and stuffing prime candidates into the upstream end.

HONEYMOON'S OVER - WHAT HAPPENED NEXT?

In the investor community, there was emerging realisation that not much was actually making its way out to market. The prospect of being lumbered with huge fixed costs if a drug failed was a serious concern. Coincidentally, during the '80s, other sectors were outsourcing 'non-core activities', claiming significant benefits in risk reduction, plus lower costs to boot. That seemed like the perfect solution.

Discovery research and marketing were considered core activities, while the drudge of running clinical trials, manufacturing and testing materials, movement and storage, making active ingredients and patient dosages were all classed as non-core.

RETURN TO THE PRINCIPALITY FOR INSPIRATION

After the Morgans' success, Evan Bevan, the village bank manager, paid the family a visit. Mr. Bevan took pride in his financial prowess that he learned from a course in the big city. He had some interesting advice for the family.

'Now that you've got all this money coming in,' he said, 'you must capitalise on it. That's what all the financial kids in the city say - money has to work for you. Now, I've been through your accounts and you have an awful lot of money tied up in these sausage machines. I also noticed that if you don't have any work going through the machines, they are lying idle. And why are you filling the sausage machine with all these products for which the prince pays us a pittance after the ten years are up?

'I'm telling you, John Morgan, this is all a big mistake. You could be using that money to find lots of different types of sausages and keep the queen and her subjects sweet. They can go on buying, and the money will keep rolling in. It's a faultless plan.'

John, David and Morfydd looked at Evan Bevan as if he were some kind of god. He was a powerful man in the village. Yet they also felt a strange foreboding in their stomachs as they contemplated the task ahead. Nearly everyone in the village worked for them as well as a significant number from the surrounding counties within the principality, but they agreed to follow the plan in the name of progress. And so the carnage began, and the unyielding pursuit of science (discovery research) began.

5 : PCs JETTISON THEIR ASSETS

OUTSOURCING BEGINS IN EARNEST

The exact sequence of events isn't easy to pin down, but the results were unmistakable — masses of workers were shown the door and thousands of facilities went up for sale.

Ousted senior execs looking for pastures new put the dumped assets to good use. They set up small companies, dubbed 'biotech' at the time, (we will call them small drug developers or SDDs,) developing drugs to either sell to Big Pharma or try to get to market themselves.

The CEOs in SDDs were making a persuasive case to be the engine house of drug discovery, citing less bureaucracy and shorter chains of command. Investors liked the sound of it and started pumping money in.

Meanwhile, other exiting senior execs joined together and bought up the facilities, funded by a different cadre of investors. These companies provided SDDs with services in exchange for a fee, under contract. These became known as contract development and manufacturing organisations (CDMOs) and contract research organisations (CROs).

Many of the rest of the redundant staff became consultants. Not the McKinsey kind - more former employees selling their skills back into the industry under contracts of varying length. I became one of them.

Also on the agenda was the tricky business of supplying hospitals and pharmacies. Handling customer complaints and dealing with ever more frequent deliveries were not deemed core and Big Pharma handed over all of its warehousing and distribution assets to gratefully receiving wholesalers.

Similarly, specialist third party logistics providers (3PLs) grew their businesses helping with the burgeoning volumes of materials and products that needed to be stored and transported around the globe.

The final arm of the strategy was 'out-throwing'; the practice of dropping existing products once the patent expired because they wouldn't meet the sumptuous ROI targets the branded versions had enjoyed.

Up sprung companies with more modest profit aspirations working to much tighter margins, copying the originals. This gave rise to the generics industry, where, at last, competition was going to save the day, or was it?

HOW DID THE DYNAMIC PAN OUT?

The number of SDDs began to accelerate as the potential rewards in doing a licensing deal with Big Pharma were immense. These new boys on the block were developing drugs themselves, hoping to eventually hand the baton on to Big Pharma.

There was similar growth in numbers for the CDMO/CROs because business was brisk as both the SDDs and Big Pharma increasingly needed their services.

The Drug Price Competition and Patent Term Restoration Act of 1984 ('The Hatch-Waxman Act') gave a welcome boost to the use of generics, and this, in turn, was more business for the CDMO/CROs.

With the growth of biologics, more companies entered the fray.

Chapter Five

Biosimilars, the generic equivalent in biologics, were attempting to capture innovator markets as patent expiry loomed. Biobetters were aiming to improve on what had gone before. Again, they needed the services of CDMO/CROs.

The ever-increasing availability of services to cover almost every aspect of drug development encouraged universities to spin out their research ideas into SDDs on the trail of Big Pharma attention and licensing deals. Government grants and funded bodies were set-up to support progress.

All this time, the contractors had begun consolidating, egged on by private equity regarding service providers as high potential, less risky investments; and all was not rosy in the PC garden.

WHERE ARE THINGS TODAY?

PCs are dried up prunes compared to the fulsome plums they used to be. They have retrenched into opposite ends of the prescription medicines lifecycle, leaving most of the work of testing, developing, making, storing, moving and distributing medicines to third parties.

On the other side of the fence, the fledgling service providers flew the nest years ago and grew into fully formed adults. Many have been soaring like eagles.

CROs have been and still are consolidating, becoming big, powerful providers of clinical and non-clinical services.

Massive consolidation has also taken place in the CDMO world, and media evidence suggests they are moving into additional areas of the value chain.

The specialist 3PLs have also been part of the consolidation as the two main players have been acquired by giant corporations, one from inside pharma and one from outside.

The finished-product distributors of pharma products are now mega corporations, on the back of – yes, you guessed it – consolidation. Just three share nearly 90% of the market on each side of the pond. There has been forward integration (pharmacies) and reverse integration (logistics specialists) going on for some time, and also moves into broader service offerings to the industry.

The generics industry has grown enormously on the back of payer demands for cheaper drugs. Up to 90% of drugs now sold in the US and UK are generic. Ironically, in later times, the intense competition for out-of-patent drugs has subsided, which has led to spiraling rises in generic drug prices. This again has been attributed to M&A activity leading to far fewer, bigger players on the field being able to pick and choose what they supply, with the ever-present shortages adding to the hikes.

This is a very different industry compared to the days prior to the Tagamet/Zantac affair. The diagram below shows how it was in those halcyon days pre-blockbusters:

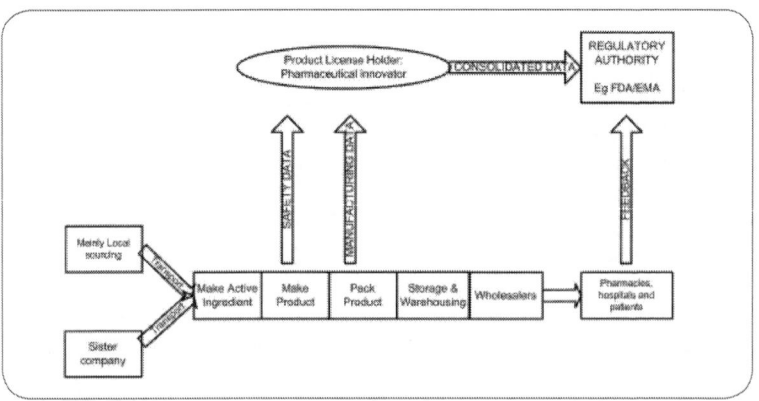

Here we see a vertically integrated arrangement where medicines are produced under one roof, made from ingredients sourced either local to the company geographically or from sister companies.

Chapter Five

Distribution is through the company country network so that customers such as community pharmacies, clinics, hospitals and other outlets could make direct contact with the manufacturer in the event of complaints or concerns.

During my 16 years at Bayer in the UK in the 1980s and 1990s, we received inter-company and mainly EU-sourced raw materials and ingredients into the goods receiving bay, they were mixed up, made into dosage forms, and packaged as finished products to be sent on their way to hospitals and pharmacies around the UK. Non-UK markets were mainly handled by shipping to other Bayer legal entities around the globe for distribution to customers.

The decision to outsource had a dramatic effect on the way PCs and the actors within the system did business. Below is a diagram showing the end-to-end supply chain stages, from raw materials to patients:

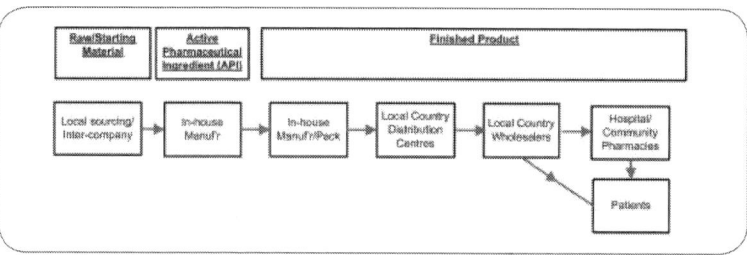

Outsourcing led to a whole new layer of complexity in the supply chain, as we see below:

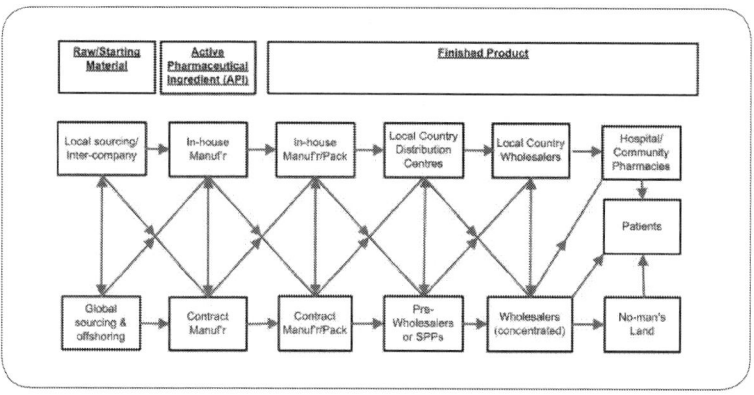

...and business models proliferated accordingly too:

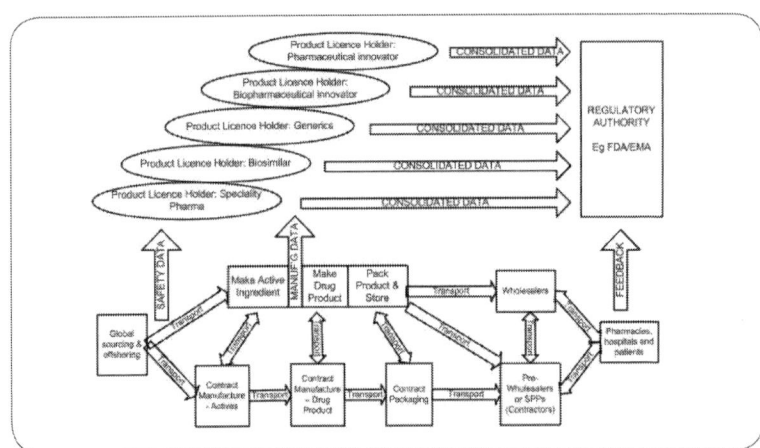

...Enter mayhem, confusion and too many cooks. How is this ever going to deliver a satisfactory broth?

DYSFUNCTIONAL MARRIAGE LEAVES ITS MARK

In 2006 the US Government Accountability Office penned a damning report on productivity levels, attrition rates and other issues in the industry. The diagram below was included in the report, having been originally created by the US industry trade association PhRMA:

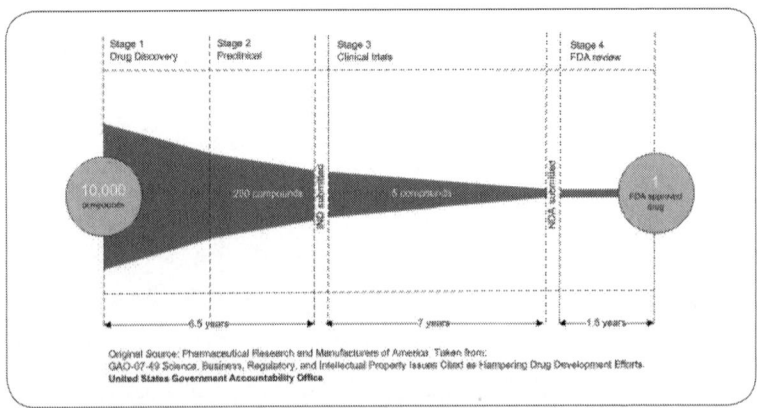

Chapter Five

SUMMING IT UP

In a nutshell, the findings were this:

- 10,000 (patented) molecules screened
- 250 undergo preclinical development and testing
- 5 enter clinical development
- 1 gains approval
- 249 development candidates fail to make it
- 4 out of 5 clinical trials fail
- It takes 10-12 years to gain approval of a development candidate
- Staggering 90%+ waste, $$$BNs in the bin

6 : PANIC AND CONFUSION REIGN IN THE INDUSTRY

"Don't panic, Captain Mainwaring!"
(Lance Corporal Jones, Dad's Army)

For those not familiar with British television's *'Dad's Army'*, Lance Corporal Jones was a Home Guard soldier during the Second World War famous for cautioning all around not to panic while exhibiting all the signs himself. He would brandish his bayonet and declare: 'They don't like it up 'em, you know,' (the enemy, that is), and implore his commanding officer, Captain Mainwaring, to set him loose among them in a brave attempt to resolve the unfolding crisis. The captain always remained calm, berated Jones for his lack of self-control and fortitude, and took matters into his own hands.

Some say the medicines industry should be panicking, à la Corporal Jones, and be ready to fix bayonets as we speak. Others are far more like the captain, refusing to be moved in the face of symptoms that might be worrying to some but which they consider mere figments of the imagination.

Corporal Jones would point toward the many pundits in the industry – prophets of doom, some might say – quoting a string of issues such as eye-watering medicine prices, dried-up product pipelines, patent 'cliffs' (with nothing to replace expiring product patents), generic competition ('copycat medicines'), tougher regulation (such as that of the FDA) and the 'valley of death' (when medicines fail to get regulatory approval). The captain would caution against jumping to rash conclusions and to look at the matter with a cool, calculating head. Accordingly, we take the captain's approach, ask the important questions on everyone's lips, and look for answers. We begin with the cost of developing a medicine.

DOES IT COST A FORTUNE TO DEVELOP A NEW MEDICINE?

Tufts University declared in November 2014 that it cost $2.6 billion to develop a medicine,[2] a 145 percent increase, correcting for inflation, over the estimate Tufts University made in 2003. That is a very big number in anyone's book.

Shortly afterward, Medecins Sans Frontieres/Doctors Without Borders rebutted the report's findings: 'if you believe that, you probably also believe the Earth is flat,' the organisation said. It quoted costs of around $50 million to develop certain medicines or up to $186 million if you took failure into account.

These are two very different assessments of the situation on the costs of medicine development. So who is right? Tufts University? Medecins Sans Frontieres? Or is neither right, and some other figure is the one to use?

There is no straight answer on this, and understandably so. It seems to depend on who you ask.

ARE SOME MEDICINES TOO EXPENSIVE?

In an article entitled 'Politicians Shouldn't Question Medicine Costs But Rather Their Value. Lessons From Soliris And Sovaldi', we hear the view of John L. LaMattina PhD, former senior vice president of Pfizer Inc. and president of Pfizer global research and development. He comments:

'It is not too surprising to see politicians now suddenly jumping on the bandwagon and expressing outrage over the cost of new medicines. Sovaldi, a medicine that essentially cures Hepatitis C, has been the subject of numerous news stories focused on its cost – $84,000 for a twelve week course of treatment.'

La Mattina argues that value, not cost, should be the yardstick. In the absence of transparency on how the cost is determined, though, it is impossible to make the balance of judgment on what is fair and whether politicians are jumping onto some kind of bandwagon, as opposed to asking the questions that need to be asked.

IS MEDICINES DEVELOPMENT REALLY A RISKY BUSINESS?

Please refer to the US GAO Report above and judge for yourself.

ARE PCs BECOMING MORE PATIENT-FOCUSSED THESE DAYS?

There is much talk these days about PCs becoming more centred on the patient, and US legislation is demanding it. The US government's '21st Century Cures Act, Title II: Patient-Focused Medicine Development', calls for greater consultation and involvement of patients in the development of medicines. There seems to be a long way to go, however. In his article 'Developing Your Patient-Centric Strategy', Richard Jones, managing director of Open Health's patient engagement agency, makes the following points:

'As a concept, "patient-centricity" — the process of designing a service or solution around the patient — is really rather simple, but as an aim for medicines companies, it is all too often overlooked.

'Yet there is no denying the increasing buzz around being patient-centric and close to the patient. Here in the UK, it has been driven by NHS thinking, such as "no decision about me, without me," and ideas around putting the patient at the heart of decision-making, and such discussions have taken root in many countries.

'Within the industry, companies often express their desire to be patient-centric organisations. Whether "inspired by patients, driven by science" (UCB); "science and patients... the heart of everything we do" (AstraZeneca); or being "a global integrated healthcare leader focused on patients' needs" (Sanofi), the industry has enthusiastically grasped the idea of patient-centricity.

'But companies such as UCB, AstraZeneca and Sanofi, like the rest of the industry, have brands and brand managers. Big Pharma's challenge is how to be truly patient-centric when their vehicle of engagement is a brand, not a disease.'

Richard makes an excellent point, and we will return to this concern over brands, not patients, later.

Investigating the question further, an excerpt from an article in the United Kingdom's *Daily Mail*, Tuesday, July 7, 2015, had this to say about PC attitudes toward patient needs:

'From simple white paracetamol to blue diamond-shaped Viagra, our pills come in all shapes, sizes, and colors.'

The conclusion from the article is that a PC does not take account of patient need because it doesn't have to. There are no specific rules it needs to follow.

We could determine from the above, then, that patient-centricity has not been a concern in the past, but there is pressure from outside to move that way.

IS THERE A LACK OF INNOVATION IN MEDICINES DEVELOPMENT?

PhRMA, the Medicines (Pharmaceutical) Research and Manufacturers of America, counters any argument that PCs lack innovation. This is what the industry body has to say on the topic:

Chapter Six

'As one of the most research-intensive and science-driven industries in the US, the pharmaceutical industry is committed to the research and development (R&D) of new treatments and cures for patients, including those who have serious unmet medical needs. With more than 7,000 innovative medicines in development worldwide by pharmaceutical companies and over $500 billion invested in R&D since 2000, hope is certainly on the horizon.'

At the same time, there are mounting complaints from a number of quarters about 'me-too' medicines. These are medicines that are approved for sale even though they are no better than the ones already on the market. One of our expert witnesses, Jack Shapiro, president of JM Shapiro Healthcare Marketing Research and Management Consulting in Maywood, NJ, had this to say:

'Too many of our medicines are basically expensive me-too medicines that offer minimal, if any, advantages over earlier compounds. Physicians know this, and patients eventually figure it out and can't understand why their doctor is making them pay so much for so little. High-tier co-pays don't help this problem.'

Who is right on this one? There appear to be thousands of medicines under development but a shortage of evidence on how many get through to make a difference in the lives of patients. Could there be some confusion in the industry over what innovation is really all about?

ARE PCs TOO SALES DRIVEN?

For an inside track on this question, we turn to an expert witness, Hanno Wolfram. I came across an article of his in *PharmaPhorum* on the topic of patient-centricity and was impressed by his insights. He has extensive experience of sales and marketing in the industry, and I asked him to share his experiences of selling in the medicines industry.

AN EXPERT WITNESS STATEMENT: MR. HANNO WOLFRAM

Q. How did Big Pharma sales-field forces operate prior to the blockbuster era?

A. In the early days of pharmaceutical field forces, those employees visiting and consulting physicians on therapeutic issues were called 'medical representatives.' Their task was to represent their company's expertise concerning the treatment of specific diseases. In these early days, medical representatives had a very clear mission statement: 'No one knows more about therapy than we do.'

Physicians had their doors wide open, and more often than not, medical representatives were welcomed with the sentence: 'Dear colleague, do you prefer coffee or tea?' Calls lasted fifteen to thirty minutes on average. The objective of that visit was simple: to answer any question a physician had. Doctors discussed their problems in scientific depth and breadth with their 'therapeutic advisors.'

Medical representatives those days fully respected that symptom assessment and diagnosis were solely and fully the clinician's domain. Finding a diagnosis was even called the art of a medical doctor. Yet vast knowledge about therapy and the ability to advise and consult physicians on the right drug to prescribe was a domain of well-trained and perfectly equipped medical representatives.

If there was any kind of 'flu, or bacterial, or viral epidemic, medical representatives gathered experiences and shared them with all of their doctors. Scientific literature and the latest publications in renowned magazines were always part of valued and valuable discussions. It was absolutely clear that, once asked, they proposed the optimal therapy. It was not at all mandatory, nor expected, that they only and always suggested 'their drug' as the best option.

Chapter Six

In those days, physicians trusted medical representatives and were seen as next of kin. Physicians were easily accessible, and medical representatives were their sources of in-depth therapeutic knowledge. Medical representatives' visits were welcome interruptions to the daily routine of asking and listening to patients. The medical representative who came, then, was the welcome listener. Clinicians could speak out, ask questions, and share everyday details at a professional level. Asking for advice from a trusted person in a confidential setting was what made medical representatives irreplaceable for many physicians, in those bygone days.

Q. What changes did you observe in Big Pharma's selling practices?

A. Big Pharma changed strategy and started to hire salespeople for their field forces. Someone had come up with the idea that 'selling' delivered more than helping physicians make the best therapeutic choices, consulting, advising, and sharing the huge pharma disease know-how with prescribers.

After 'selling' as a technical term had been established, the era of the 'race of arms' started. The more representatives you had, the faster you could achieve market penetration. The dose-response curve had been copied from the research people. Consultants called it the 'S-curve'. The more calls in a certain time, in the shortest possible frequency per physician, the higher the revenue, until the 'S' flattened out to a point of diminishing return.

From fast-moving consumer goods companies, Big Pharma learned the utmost importance of 'knowing thy customer.' This finding included the introduction of the word 'customer.' Today, almost every touch-point pharma might have is named 'customer.' Once the term 'customer' was widely used, customer relationship management was born. Today, customer relationship management has widely degenerated to a policing tool of a representative's activities and prerequisite for analysis, often showing little practical or managerial relevance.

This selling vocabulary for Big Pharma coined a mentality and led to laws and codes of conduct – and simultaneously pharma's ideas to circumvent them. A number of anti-corruption laws originate from pharma's 'selling skills', especially from the step called 'closing the deal'. Growing sales became the core objective and key performance indicator in pharma. Yet being sales driven started to result in legal trials, prison sentences and billion dollar fines.

After these painful selling attempts, the majority of the target group today says: 'No, there is no value seeing a pharma salesperson.' More and more access restrictions are subsequently imposed. In some countries, more than 50 percent of all prescribers have fully closed their doors to pharma.

DO PCs TURN A BLIND-EYE TO SIDE EFFECTS?

An article by Laura Donnelly and Edward Malnick for the UK's *Daily Telegraph* reported on the United Kingdom's National Health Service's advice that there should be widespread use of statins:

'The advice has divided experts, with prominent doctors accusing NICE's (National Institute for Health and Care Excellence) experts of being too close to the pharmaceutical industry.'

Debate has raged for some time over the risks and benefits of taking a statin every day. The proponents of statins argue that lower cholesterol levels serve to reduce the overall risk of heart problems in the over 55s population, whereas the opponents do not accept patients should be exposed to the potential side effects unless there is a properly diagnosed need.

One general practitioner describes the side effects as 'horrific' and a large percentage refuse to follow the advice, even though they could be financially penalised by not following NICE's dictate.

Aside from the statins debate, the industry has a less-than-stellar record for being truthful about safety profiles of drugs, as

Chapter Six

evidenced by 'Vioxx', which has left a bitter taste in the mouths of many families and doctors affected. For those not familiar with the story, Merck gained US FDA approval to launch the painkiller Vioxx (rofecoxib) in 1999 based upon clinical trial evidence.

Following launch, there emerged a growing body of evidence that the drug was implicated in heart attacks and death. As the *Drugwatch* website reported: 'In the years that followed, it was mired in scandal. Merck was accused of misleading doctors and patients about the drug's safety, fabricating study results to suit the company's needs, continually thwarting an FDA scientist from revealing the drug's problems and skirting federal drug regulations.' During this time, patients were dying.

Campaigns have been started to achieve far greater visibility of safety profiles and other critical issues involved in clinical trials. In his book *Bad Pharma*, physician Ben Goldacre reveals astonishing insights into the workings of the industry.

None of this, however, seems to be persuading PCs to change.

ARE COPYCAT MEDICINES (GENERICS/BIOSIMILARS) THE SAME AS THE ORIGINAL?

We start with an expert witness, Richard Meyer, a LinkedIn member of my discussion group, Friends of Modernisation in the Drug Industry. He is also a prolific writer about the industry, particularly with respect to marketing practices.

Richard will pitch in here with a snippet from one of his frequent reports on industry issues.

Q. Tell us a little bit about concerns that generic drugs are not the same as originals.

A. I had the chance yesterday to be on the *Huffington Post Live* to discuss generic drugs in the wake of the article by *Fortune* on

'Ranbaxy'. Not surprisingly, a lot of people chimed in and had concerns about generic drugs, which is no surprise considering that the FDA's definition of bioequivalence is surprisingly broad: a generic's maximum concentration of active ingredient in the blood must not fall more than 20 percent below or 25 percent above that of the brand name. This means a potential range of 45 percent by that measure, among generics labeled as being the same.

There are other differences. The generic must contain the same active ingredient as the original. But the additional ingredients, known as excipients, can be different and are often of lower quality. Those differences can affect what's called bioavailability— the amount of drug that could potentially be absorbed into the bloodstream. As the American Heart Association recently noted, 'Some additives traditionally thought to be inert, such as alcohol sugars, cyclodextrans, and polysorbate-80, may alter a drug's dissolution, thereby impacting its bioavailability.'

The FDA standards also do not specifically regulate how quickly the medicine reaches peak concentration in the blood. That can become a major issue for patients who take generic versions of time-release drugs, which constitute ten percent of the market, according to IMS Health. The time-release mechanisms for branded drugs are usually protected by separate patents, so generics companies engineer alternative and usually cheaper mechanisms.

That can result in drugs that release active ingredients into the blood far more quickly, leaving patients feeling dizzy or nauseated. Barbara Davit, director of the Division of Bioequivalence II in the FDA's Office of Generic Drugs, acknowledges that the agency does not apply 'formal statistics' to measuring 'Tmax- the time it takes for a drug to reach maximum concentration. But reviewers do informally consider it, she says, asserting that applications have been rejected because of Tmax results.

Chapter Six

Q. Interesting, Richard. What do you think empowered patients are going to think about this information? Are they going to believe it, or are they going to see a sinister conspiracy by the drug industry to throw mud on generic drugs?

A. I worked in the generic drug industry for over-the-counter products and can tell you that there are differences between branded drugs and generics. Are those differences worth an 85 percent price premium? Probably not, but drug companies would be smart to lower prices of branded drugs significantly when their product comes off patent. Physicians should also listen to patient complaints about side effects after they have been switched to generics and to monitor outcomes of generics versus branded drugs.

There is also further evidence from *FiercePharma's* web report titled 'FDA Quietly Testing Some Drugs Generic Equivalency' which states: 'An independent study of generic versions of Pfizer's cholesterol-lowering drug "Lipitor" done by Preston Mason at Brigham & Women's Hospital, found some of the generics were ineffective because of impurities resulting from the manufacturing.'

I have been told by some of the world's greatest authorities on the manufacture of drugs, during discussions in my Friends of Modernisation in the Drug Industry LinkedIn group, that the non-active ingredients (excipients) that go into making the tablet or other dosage form can seriously affect the performance of the drug. Not all, but there are some well-known cases where this has happened, and probably others that have not come to light. I am told that the testing of a generic to prove equivalence with the original medicines industry product does not identify these differences. To me, that is a big issue because patients tend to be unaware of this and there is so much pressure to move patients toward generic versions to save costs.

There is also an irony in that the medicines development approval process does not allow the generic company access to non-active ingredients in the original formula when, as we learned above, these can have an important effect on a drug's performance.

We move on now to another high-profile question.

WHY IS TESTING IN ANIMALS STILL A WIDELY HELD PRACTICE?

The BBC reported on June 4, 2015 the European Union's decision to declare that it was not possible to develop medicines without testing in animals. During the debate leading up to the decision, the British trade body had this to say:

'While the UK's bio-medicines industry says it is committed to reducing and ultimately replacing the use of animals for scientific research, "this is not yet possible due to the complexity of the interactions between cells, tissues, and organs in the body, which cannot yet be fully modeled in vitro or by computers," Dr. Virginia Acha, ABPI executive director for Research Medical and Innovation, told CNBC via e-mail.'

On the other hand, Stop Vivisection, the group responsible for the petition, argues that animal testing has hindered development of alternative biomedical research methods and poses a danger to human health and the environment. On its website, the organisation says that existing provisions allow for testing on stray cats and dogs.

More conflicting opinions prevent us from drawing a conclusion. We finish here with my own specialty subject: the end-to-end medicines supply chain.

WHAT IS GOING ON IN THE MEDICINES SUPPLY CHAIN?

Many from outside the industry, and more from inside, are unfamiliar with operations in the medicines industry supply chain

Chapter Six

in recent years. These typically appear under the categories of economically motivated adulteration, shortages, counterfeiting, and cargo diversion/theft.

Economically motivated adulteration first hit the news in 2007 when a toxic ingredient was found in 'Heparin', (a blood-thinning agent), supplied by Baxter. It resulted in reports of 574 adverse events, nine patient deaths and hundreds injured. Investigators discovered that Baxter had procured raw materials from a rogue source. The source saved costs by using what turned out to be a toxic substance. Suddenly, economically motivated adulteration was a term on everyone's lips. After the incident, Pew Charitable Trust released an excellent, in-depth report titled 'After Heparin'.

This is the summary of the situation from Pew:

'In late 2007, US health officials began receiving reports of unexpected allergic-type reactions in patients undergoing dialysis. The reactions were linked to a widely used blood thinner – Heparin – and specifically to an adulterant that had been introduced during manufacture of the drug in China. The US Food and Drug Administration (FDA) believes the adulteration of Heparin was an economically motivated act – a clear breach of the US drug's supply chain.

'Drug manufacturers and distributors work together in a robust system to deliver high quality products, but drug manufacturing and distribution have become increasingly complex in recent years. Prescription and over-the-counter (OTC) medications originate in factories all over the world, moving into the American marketplace through supply chains that can involve numerous processing plants, manufacturers, suppliers, brokers, packagers, and distributors.

'The number of drug products made outside of the United States doubled from 2001 to 2008, according to FDA estimates. The FDA estimates that up to 40 percent of finished drugs used by US patients are manufactured abroad, and 80 percent of active ingredients and bulk chemicals used in US drugs come from foreign countries. Increasingly, the United States relies on drug manufacturing in developing countries – mainly China and India. Globalisation, increased outsourcing of manufacturing, the complexity of drug distribution, and the existence of criminal actors willing to capitalise on supply chain weaknesses has created the potential for counterfeit or substandard medicines to enter the system and reach patients. As evidenced by the adulteration of Heparin and other case studies outlined in this report, these rare but potentially serious events can have grave consequences.'

Product shortages in the supply chain attracted the attention of the US government, and on October 31, 2011, President Barack Obama signed an executive order directing the FDA to take action to reduce prescription drug shortages which the White House said had endangered patients and led to price gouging. He explained the reason for the order:

'Recently, we have seen how the potential of drug shortages for vital drugs, including some cancers, can really have an adverse impact on patients and those who are caring for patients. Sometimes we run out of or run low on certain types of drugs, and that drives up prices and it increases patient risk,' President Obama said at the signing in the Oval Office.

'The executive order instructs the FDA to take action in three areas: broaden reporting of potential drug shortages, expedite regulatory reviews that can help prevent shortages, and examine whether potential shortages have led to illegal price gouging.

*'Over the last five years, the number of these drug shortages has nearly tripled. Even though the FDA has prevented an actual crisis, this is one of those slow-rolling problems that could end up resulting in disaster for patients and healthcare facilities all across the country. Congress has been trying since February to

do something about this. It has not yet been able to get it done, and it is the belief of this administration... that we can't wait for action on The Hill. We've got to go ahead and move forward.'

We see here that concern over supply-chain issues moved even the US president into action.

Similar issues have been taking place in the European Union, albeit the finished product shortage issue had its roots in a different dynamic than the United States. This was driven largely by what is known as 'parallel trade'. Drugs that have been bought by an intermediary in a lower-price EU country are repackaged in the new language and then resold in the higher-price EU market. It resulted in those buying products from the medicines manufacturers, such as pharmacies and even hospitals, ordering above their needs from the manufacturers to sell on to the repackagers and make a better return than they were getting from the healthcare system in their own country. Unlike in the United States, there has been no opportunity to legislate because the practice is legal under EU competition laws and, in fact, the parallel traders are awarded licenses to do it.

AN EXPERT WITNESS STATEMENT: CATHERINE GEYMAN

Q. What do you make of the shortages issue?

A. The (lack of) resilience of global pharmaceutical supply chain networks has been laid bare in recent years by the global drug shortage crisis mentioned above, which peaked in 2011. As with any systemic supply-chain issue, the causes are numerous and complex, but they tend to hub around self-imposed cost-reduction initiatives removing the historical slack in supply chains' ability to absorb the impact of quality deviations. This increasing pressure in the industry to become more cost effective has led to initiatives such as blanket safety-stock reduction, removing any slack in the supply chain.

In some cases, stock is there for a very good reason: to mitigate a significant single-source dependency or protect a product launch from forecast uncertainties. When taken away, it can result in severe issues in response to unplanned events.

Q. What other effects have you seen from cost-reduction efforts?

A. A company's asset base may also have suffered from the sharpening of the accountant's pencil. The removal of redundant capacity can also result in disruption being felt in the marketplace. Also, outsourcing to countries with immature regulatory regimes is another manifestation of the cost-reduction drive. The unhappy side effect of this has been the accompanying decrease in quality standards.

Separate European and US root cause analyses of the acute drug shortages were carried out in 2011/12, and the general consensus was that quality problems were the biggest contributors to the shortages. Unsurprisingly, the low-cost suppliers that can demonstrate superior quality standards have attracted the large customers, and the net result is a concentration of risk on certain contract manufacturers. This leaves a proportion of the industry vulnerable not only to the ongoing viability of certain suppliers, but in some cases exposed to the increased threat of natural hazards and political instabilities that are part of the package.

Q. Who else has had a part to play in this?

A. The regulators have also played their part in both the problem and the solution. Regulatory interventions were a contributory factor to the acute shortages of 2011-12 when a number of major manufacturers voluntarily shut down to correct systemic quality failings and the marketplace simply didn't have the capacity to fill the gap. However, following some high-profile finger pointing, the regulators are playing a much more positive role in resolving drug shortages by not enforcing recalls of certain drugs that were already in short supply, fast-tracking new products, and allowing products in from other markets.

Chapter Six

Q. Has industry consolidation played a part?

A. The industry's manufacturing base is being consolidated through takeover. Mergers and acquisitions inevitably result in rationalisation of assets, in particular where the merging companies were previously selling substantially similar products. The net result is a global marketplace with fewer sourcing options.

Q. What risks do you see that remain lurking in pharma supply chains?

A. By way of example of the range of risks and issues facing the pharma supply base:

- Tight margins rule the chemical, food, and widget suppliers, making them particularly susceptible to the economic cycle. The 2008 economic crisis saw key pharma polymer suppliers hit financially, (particularly by the downturn in the automotive industry), resulting in idling of plants and a reduction in the already constrained supply base. Furthermore, pharma companies often present an unattractive prospect with their low volume requirements and exacting specifications, making relationship building to mitigate the risks a challenge.

- Certain biologics products that depend on living things as a fundamental feedstock can also be a cause for many a supply chain manager's sleepless nights. While the originators of specific cells such as cattle are closely controlled and often isolated from the food supply chain, they are nonetheless vulnerable to infectious disease and even to benign cell contamination that can manifest itself quietly during development and only rear its ugly head post-commercialisation.

- Specialist delivery device manufacturers are often unique, sole sources and very difficult to replace. It's not only the exacting specification of a device or material that can make finding an alternative challenging; it is also necessary that the downstream validation batches, (evidence that the manufacturer can achieve the required standard), can make the time to establish an alternative source in several months rather than weeks.

- This leads on to some of the limitations that the industry has been known to place on itself such as naming a specific supplier or a particular supplier's grade of material in the regulatory dossier, making the prospect of changing suppliers or establishing alternatives in an emergency a potentially time-consuming process.
- The industry also has a fundamental fear of the regulator and, consequently, any changes/improvements to a validated process tend to be few and far between. This also has implications for finding alternative sources of supply should things go wrong, which makes recovering from any supply chain disruptions a lengthy process.

Counterfeit medicines have also found their way into the legitimate supply chain for medical products, with the potential to harm, maim, and kill patients. Here are just two examples:

- As of March 31, 2014, counterfeits of Pfizer's medicines have been found in 107 countries and breached the legitimate supply chain in sixty countries.
- In April, 2014, falsified vials of the breast cancer treatment 'Herceptin' were found in Europe after Herceptin vials had been stolen in Italy and undergone tampering.

In 2011, the European Union passed the 'Falsified Medicines Directive', leading to major revisions to the laws of good distribution practice and some revisions to good manufacturing practice, including a requirement for track-and-trace on certain higher-risk finished products. In the United States, the 'FDA Safety and Innovation Act' became law, again with the intention of cracking down on illicit activities in the supply chain, as well as encouraging better working practices. More recently, the FDA has

Chapter Six

penned the 'Drug Supply Chain Security Act'. Similarly to the European Union, it calls for track-and-trace to be implemented, albeit to a less-challenging timetable than the EU's.

Where does all this panic and confusion leave us?

MORGANS CONCLUDE SAUSAGES AREN'T QUITE AS SUCCULENT AS THEY WERE

John Morgan came to the farmhouse dinner table with a grim look on his face.

'What's going on?' Morfydd inquired. *'What did Mister Bevan say?'*

'Oh, the usual. He wanted to know where we are with the new succulent sausages on the go. He's getting a lot of heat from his people at the bank.'

Morfydd pressed her luck a little further. *'Did you tell him what had happened to the latest range we sent for sampling?'*

'Of course I didn't. Do you think I'm mad? He'd go ballistic if he knew they didn't go down well with the samplers. We just need more time to come up with some answers.'

David knew his mother could venture no further. He decided to continue with the questioning himself.

'What IS happening though, Dad? Are we losing our touch, or is something else going on?'

John Morgan took a more conciliatory tone with his only son.

'I'm as baffled as you are, David. We seem to be doing all the same things we did in the early days – it's just the succulent sausages aren't coming through.'

Taming the Big Pharma Monster

David looked thoughtfully at his father and asked the first of a number of questions that had been bothering him for some time.

'Do you think we were right to sell off the sausage machines, Dad?'

'I know what you mean, son. Since they have been contracting to us, they seem to have stopped trying. Each time we want to develop a new sausage, the first question is how much will we pay to develop it?

'We can't do it on our own anymore, and they know that. And if no sausages come out at the end, it's no skin off their nose.'

Neither was in the mood to laugh at the unintended pun, and Morfydd didn't want to risk it when John was in this mood.

David inquired further. 'Why didn't we keep making the sausages when the queen's special period ran out? The companies making copies of our old ones seem to be doing wonderful trade, and all are making good profits.'

'I know, I know, David. Don't you think I haven't thought about that?' said John, irritation closing in even with his blue-eyed boy.

Then David asked: 'What about all these small guys that have sprung up and are offering to sell us part-finished sausages they claim to be succulent, using our former sausage machines to do it?

'When we've bought them, they didn't fit properly into the sausage machine we use, and the data wasn't as good as they said. And the other thing, Dad – these days it's costing us a king's ransom to keep the queen and her subjects on board with our sausages to hold the competition out.'

Chapter Six

'We're in a different ball game now, David. There are more and more different types of aversion to the vegetarian diet that need a protein supplement, and there's our opportunity, if you ask me.

'If we can find a cure for some of these rare conditions, we can be in a position to make a lot of money again. True, they are a lot pickier about cows getting tummy upsets, and the same with the rest of the sampling system, but if we keep throwing pork at it, we're sure to get there in the end, aren't we?'

David, still not convinced, made the next point:

'Along with this, as I said earlier, we are struggling to get the attention of all these contractors. They have lots of new clients now developing sausages of their own. We have to pay them a lot of money to work on our trials and make the sausages for us. We have to keep everything secret from them in case they start making our sausages themselves. Do you really think we can go on like this, Dad?'

"I don't know" is the simple answer, David, but I can't see what else we can do other than keep plugging away at it.'

David nodded thoughtfully and said: 'We've got to think of something Dad, and fast, otherwise we won't be in the sausage business this time next year'

7 : WHAT ARE THE HARSH REALITIES FOR PCs?

So what went wrong along the way?

In terms of the our latest instalment above, the mega returns of the early days have stalled. The bank of molecule 'chips', replenished and systematically placed on the roulette wheel of regulatory review, has dried up.

When the odds began to go against it, facilities and people were cast out to conserve the stash in the bank. As the odds continued to favour the house, resources were funneled into discovery research and sales and marketing. Development increasingly became the poor relation, taken for granted as the necessary evil to be overcome on the road to life in the sun.

This, of course, has been the fatal mistake. Development covers the entire product-development cycle, from conceptualisation to commercialisation. The early successes in pharma struck the industry blind to the true nature of what it was doing. The industry is still blind to it. That is why this is the overriding harsh reality. The industry, and Big Pharma, in particular, is an addict in denial, still placing its bets on the regulatory roulette wheel.

This may seem an extreme assessment, and in some ways it is, because Big Pharma companies are still relatively rich. However, the industry's key players do exhibit many of the characteristics of the gambler: an obsession with chasing the big win (blockbusters); low-level engagement in key relationships, (for example: patients, doctors, contractors, regulators, and distributors); divestment of life possessions to fund the stake and hedge the uncertainty, (mass, tactical outsourcing, and abandonment of out-of-patent products); and a mind-set embedded in those early years of success, rather than the hard yards of working for a living.

If we take the metaphor at face value, things don't look good for Big Pharma companies because habits of a lifetime die hard. Often, addiction is a slow downward spiral into the gutter. Some would argue that that is the trajectory before us, the logical conclusion of a lifetime of neglect. It would be perfectly reasonable to see it that way given what we now know.

If the addict were to accept his plight, acknowledge the problem, and seek rehabilitation, there would be further harsh realities to face that stem from the lifetime of addiction. These need to be unearthed to appreciate the scope of the journey ahead, if it is to be one of recovery. We explore them in the remainder of this chapter.

BIG PHARMA NEEDS A SCIENCE LESSON

Science is at the core of the industry – the lion's roar - and on that front is a two-part lesson:

First, in the commercial world, science is impotent if not partnered with the translational methods in the world of engineering. Together, they travel from a good idea to a product in the hands of end users.

Second, far too little science is applied in the early stage of 'File It.' I will explain more because I suspect industry stalwarts will be up in arms at this point.

Important though science is in any endeavour, we don't dwell on the physics or thermodynamics involved in flight, nor the science of the internal combustion engine, nor any other product that ends up on the market. We know it must have been there, but that's it. 'Ah, but the human body is a million times more complex than an aircraft or a car,' they declare. 'Medicine is different.'

Chapter Seven

Yes to the first point - no to the second. Making medicine is no different. There is so much we don't understand about the sky, yet we make aircraft, rockets, and satellites by accepting the unknowns and working around them. Whether the sky is less complex than the human body, who knows? That is academic. Humans will probably never understand either.

Developing medicines for humans is no different. Yes, there is science in deciding what molecular structures could target particular disease mechanisms and receptors, but the dreadful attrition rates tell us this is something of a blunt instrument. Remember, 249 out of 250 scientific theories were wrong, and it took years to discover that.

Ironically, where science could really provide a return on investment, it is not applied. There is a tremendous need to use the latest scientific advances in predictive technologies at the point where development candidates are chosen to enter a development programme. Much can be achieved these days in predicting issues, using computer simulation and testing in animal and human tissue, for example, in silico and ex vivo techniques. Sadly, the prospect of getting into clinical trials attracts far more attention, and the valley of death is about to claim another victim.

This is why I am arguing that Big Pharma needs a lesson in science.

Systems thinking expert Peter Checkland makes this point nicely with his 'soft systems methodology'. Science is a vitally important discipline in which, as Checkland[3] puts it, 'the highest value attaches to the advancement of knowledge.' Scientists are trained to use reductionist thinking: running experiments and drawing conclusions from them. Checkland compares this way of working with the mind-set of engineers and technologists, who 'prize most highly the efficient accomplishment of some defined purpose.'

He provides an example of his work in the science-based *Imperial Chemical Industries*. His team was charged with developing synthetic leather to seize a market opportunity. A research scientist gave the project a negative response. Checkland reports his comment: 'The three dimensional matrix of natural leather is so complex that it cannot at present be accurately described. Therefore, we cannot hope to simulate it.'

The research scientist assumed that the question was about furthering scientific knowledge. Checkland's observation was: 'Had [the scientist] assumed the question to be a technological one, he would have asked not "can we copy leather?" but "can we imagine a material which will perform satisfactorily in end users' hands in which natural leather is now used?"' The search is then totally different. It is about finding an alternative solution to an end user's problem.

This is a vitally important distinction when developing products. How many companies are studying their molecules and materials rather than developing solutions for patients? We know from the US GAO figures that, on average, they are studying 10,000 molecules for every one that gets to market.

Here, then, we argue that Big Pharma companies are selecting compounds (development candidates) to register for sale when they have no idea about their chances of success. We are not saying they should be certain, because nothing in life is, but they should make a sufficient attempt to thoroughly check the robustness of the candidate for the rigors ahead - the journey through the valley of death.

Daniel Steenstra, the Royal Academy of Engineering's visiting professor of medical innovation at Cranfield University, reinforces this message.

Daniel is a qualified medic working in the field of engineering. I had contacted him via LinkedIn to ask whether he would be interested in working with me on a funding bid focused on advanced manufacturing supply chain in life science for Oxford BioMedica. He called me a few weeks later.

The bid was successful and raised £7.1 million ($11 million) from the UK government to work in the important field of gene therapy manufacturing. Daniel's views on science and innovation are spot-on, from my perspective. Here is what he has to say on the matter:

AN EXPERT WITNESS STATEMENT: PROFESSOR DANIEL STEENSTRA

Q. How would you sum up the Big Pharma approach to product development?

A. Pharma might spend lots of money on R&D, but the evidence suggests that it is simply not effective. Take the astronomical attrition rates, or the years it takes from the discovery of the new compound to market launch. New pharmaceuticals such as monoclonal antibodies or genetic therapies take decades. Other sectors are far more driven by the end users and have developed a set of processes to meet their customers' needs, such as concurrent engineering, rapid prototyping, lean manufacturing that are yet to be used in the Pharma sector. It's time that the pharma companies stop doing the wrong things, take their heads out of the sand and look around at how other companies do it.

Q. Can you tell us something about the attitude to innovation you have experienced?

A. Many companies and individuals are still confused about innovation and still think it's about creativity - coming up with new ideas. That's only the beginning. Innovation is the successful commercialisation of a new idea. That means it's the blood, sweat, and tears that turn ideas into benefits - making money from it or delivering better and higher-quality healthcare.

Innovation needs new ideas. It needs research and development to create and develop these ideas further into new products or services.

Q. So what are scientific ideas to innovation, then?

A. To use the old chicken-and-egg metaphor: the seeds (as in chicken feed) are the creative ideas, the egg is the successful outcome, the innovation. The chicken is the organisation that with its R&D, sales and marketing, manufacturing and supply chain processes turns the 'feed' into 'eggs'.

Furthermore, there are different types of innovation:

- Incremental innovation - the small changes and updates that make a product a little faster, lighter, cheaper, or of better quality.
- Radical innovation - based on a technology that has never been used, such as the first CT scan combing X-ray with computer technology.
- Disruptive innovation - the based on a simplifying technology that requires less skill and can be applied in a more convenient environment, such as a drug-eluting stent rather than coronary bypass surgery.

In reality, the pharmaceutical sector is more complex than the chicken and the egg.

In my experience, R&D in the pharma sector is very much uppercase 'R' and lowercase 'd.' It is too focused on the compound or the new pharmaceutical technology itself and ignores who is going to use it, where and how it will be applied, and who will pay for it. It has too much technology push, rather than consumer (patient or healthcare professional) pull.

Chapter Seven

THE VALLEY OF DEATH IS STEALING OUR DRUGS

So the point Daniel makes is that scientific invention — a good idea — is not an innovation until it becomes a product in the end user's hands.

Now we turn to the beast that is snapping up all the inventions and ideas.

The Charge of the Light Brigade

Half a league, half a league,
Half a league onward,
All in the valley of Death
Rode the six hundred.
'Forward, the Light Brigade!
Charge for the guns!' he said.
Into the valley of Death
Rode the six hundred.

'Forward, the Light Brigade!'
Was there a man dismay'd ?
Not tho' the soldier knew
Someone had blunder'd:
Theirs not to make reply,
Theirs not to reason why,
Theirs but to do and die.
Into the valley of Death
Rode the six hundred.

In his famous poem, Alfred Lord Tennyson describes soldiers embarking on a suicide mission, totally unaware of the wall of fire they are to face. '"Charge for the guns!" he said' - their superiors ordered the charge. 'Not tho' the soldier knew, Someone had blunder'd.' Someone had certainly blundered, and in Big Pharma the same blunder continues to be repeated. Compounds are entering the development pipeline completely unprepared for the rigours ahead, and the cannons have become bigger and louder over the years as regulators demand ever-higher standards from the industry and governments look for value for money from their healthcare budgets. What is driving this, then?

The patent clock is running the show

The motivation for the charge Lord Tennyson described was the dreadful imperative of war. What is it now for Big Pharma? It is the crack of the starting pistol once the patent clock has been set.

Somewhere during the 'Find It' stage, the company registers the molecule with the patent office. This sets a definite date for expiration of the patent-protection umbrella. The patent clock is now ticking. Every day spent on selecting a development candidate to head for the valley, and every day spent on 'File It', is a day lost to sales in the market in the minds of all involved – assuming, of course, that it gets to market. Given the statistic above, there is only a one in 250 chance of the molecule getting to market, so there is little appetite for spending time or money on its future. Everyone waits to see what the clinical data will look like some five to ten years later.

The harsh reality here is more of haste and less of speed. In the frantic effort to get into the clinic as quickly as possible, Pharma does not take the time to select its runners carefully. The more runners there are, the thinking goes, the greater the likelihood that one of them will get through the process.

As the valley becomes deeper and wider, Big Pharma has become increasingly less equipped to make the journey because of the emaciated state of its 'File It' capability, which is now predominantly in the hands of third parties or strangers, as we go on to explore.

Strangers are sailing the ship

To do justice to this next reality, I start with an expert witness, Professor Andrew Cox. The professor is world-renowned in strategic procurement and outsourcing practices and, in my estimation, is the only academic who truly understands the nature of the business of procuring goods and services from third parties. He is in great demand across all industrial sectors and has kindly offered his views here on practices in the pharma industry.

AN EXPERT WITNESS STATEMENT: Professor Andrew Cox

Q. Is Big Pharma alone in adopting less-than-optimal practices in outsourcing?

A. Many industries have extensive experience of less-than-optimal make-versus-buy decision-making and outsourcing, and the major pharmaceutical companies are no different in this respect. Most poor practice arises from low levels of professional competence and a lack of rigorous and robust make-versus-buy and outsourcing management methodologies. (Readers wishing to dig deeper can find more at 'Strategic Outsourcing & Critical Asset Management, IIAPS White Paper 15/3', www.iiaps.org, and Andrew Cox, *Sourcing Portfolio Analysis*, 2014).

Q. What is your perspective on pharma specifically?

A. In the last few decades, the major pharmaceutical companies appear to have been influenced by a number of factors when outsourcing many of their former key internal resources and capabilities (critical assets) to the suppliers in its supply chains.

The key factors appear to have been:

- a desire for more flexible use of assets
- lower perceived costs of external (developing country) supply
- short-term headcount cost reduction targets to meet quarterly financial targets
- copying the latest fad.

Q. I can see your first bullet could be for strategic reasons, but the other three appear to be based on ill-informed decision making. Is that right?

A. I'm glad you raised the point and of course you are right. The remaining three bullets reflect incompetence in the make-versus-buy decision, and knock-on management issues that can occur once the contract is signed, normally caused by three major factors:

- Unforeseen loss of critical assets. By this, I mean inadvertent outsourcing of assets that provide the basis for differentiating your product from the competition.

- Unforeseen post-contractual moral hazard. This may sound a difficult concept, but in fact it is easily explained. It means that once the contract is signed, there is a shift in the power and leverage position of the buyer and supplier over time. I sometimes lightheartedly use the analogy of my marriage contract with Mrs. Cox and how our power and leverage positions have changed over time.

- Inability to drive improvement in the supply and value chain. This last point relates to the relative weakening of a buyer's position so that it cannot drive through the necessary improvement work that is going to make them more competitive in the market. More powerful suppliers will not be obliged to offer up improved quality, reduced costs or end-user value enhancements in the end-to-end value stream unless there is a consequent return for them. If the contract assures their return anyway, then more often than not it does not make business sense for suppliers to offer things up.

Q. What evidence have you to offer from your professional expertise in this area?

A. Unfortunately for the major pharmaceutical companies that used to be the 'channel captains' who controlled the industry and all of its major supply chains through a judicious control internally of critical assets, there has been considerable evidence of very poor practice in outsourcing in recent years. This has led to the loss of critical assets, post-contractual moral hazard and poor post-contractual management of suppliers. Evidence of this poor practice is listed below:

Unforeseen loss of critical assets:

- There has been a loss of internal intellectual property (IP) and technical design, manufacturing and quality-control competencies, with growing dependency on suppliers for these key competencies.

Unforeseen post-contractual moral hazards:

- There has been an increase in regulatory and supply-chain complexity, with increased threats to corporate reputation and litigation.
- There has been an increasing and unanticipated dependency on supply-chain partnerships with distributors and manufacturers.
- There has been a failure to predict the size of switching-costs and high exit barriers to Big Pharma companies changing their key suppliers.

Inability to drive value-for-money improvement in the supply and value chain:

- There has been increasing evidence of poor quality control and adulteration of raw materials, products, and services across the industry.
- There is widespread evidence of poor schedule compliance and on-time delivery.
- The major pharmaceutical companies have been experiencing rising rather than falling prices and total costs of ownership.
- There is considerable evidence that the major pharmaceutical companies still lack cross-functional supply-chain value and process-optimisation competence.

Q. How would you sum up all of this?

A. All of these recent developments lead to a serious questioning of the strategic outsourcing undertaken by the major pharmaceutical companies in the recent past. Not only has there been an inadvertent loss of critical assets, but also an increase in competition and a loss of control of key suppliers and supply chains. Unfortunately, this has occurred at a time when competition from generic companies has increased and when profits from patented products have been in decline. The result has been an industry experiencing widespread decline in profitability, now responding with short-term, knee-jerk merger and acquisition strategies. This is a telling indictment of the failure of strategic outsourcing in the pharmaceutical industry.

These are powerful words and should send a chill through the hearts of industry executives.

There is so much for readers to pick up on here, and I hope the issues shine through. The key harsh reality I want to follow up is Professor Cox's comment: *"Major pharmaceutical companies that used to be the "channel captains"."*

This is why this section is titled 'Strangers Are Sailing The Ship'. We can confidently say that no other industry has outsourced its critical assets to the extent Big Pharma has. It has now lost the ability to design and develop its products because suppliers and contractors hold the key - and it has become a golden key for them.

Boeing dabbled with increased levels of outsourced development for the 'Dreamliner' and suffered a reported eighteen-month delay, as well as much pain and suffering, for its troubles. This is what Peter S. Cohan reported in his book *You Can't Order Change: Lessons from Jim McNerney's Turnaround at Boeing* (Hard cover, December 26, 2008): 'By outsourcing both the design and the manufacturing, Boeing lost control of the development process.' The point McNerney makes is that outsourcing manufacture can work so long as the development process and control are in the hands of the developer and the developer allows detailed instructions and specifications to be handed down to contractors and suppliers. This has not been the case for a long time in pharma. The knowledge, experience, and capabilities all lie within the supply base.

If I were to appear on British television's *Mastermind* quiz show, this would be my specialty subject. I've been involved in procuring almost every good and service pharma could ever want, from molecular modeling software to third-party, finished-goods, channel distribution services across global markets and everything in between. Through the years, I have seen the pharma purchasers get ever more locked into their contractor supply bases, and this is why. When the industry decided to mass outsource, it did not take account of the regulatory environment in which it operated. This environment prevents any company from using a contractor unless that contractor has been registered as part of the regulatory filing. The result is that any company in the filing, especially if it is the only one, is in a powerful position because the switching costs and regulatory turmoil would be enormous.

Now in the power position, contractors often are able to name their prices and charge for every little piece of work. I was at a large contract manufacturer where one of the senior executives recounted how a client complained about having to pay for the number of investigations and corrective actions. The client was charged for putting things right when they went wrong at the contractor's premises.

There is a massive gulf between healthcare professionals and Big Pharma

Even if Big Pharma remained the channel captain, there would be a further intractable obstacle in the way of taking hold of the effort to develop medicine for patients: the massive gulf between Big Pharma and the end users of its products - healthcare professionals.

This harsh reality is about the distance between companies developing drugs and the end users. The most contact drug developers have with healthcare providers is between the developing company's clinical group, (often a contract research organisation), and the clinical trial study investigators who operate within a network of hospitals and clinics signed up for the trials. The communication is pretty much one way; the investigator role is to collect data from recruits on the clinical trial. The developer has to give a brochure telling the investigator everything about the product undergoing the testing. The objective is to collect the clinical data until the end of the study, normally blind to both the investigator and patient for Phase II studies and beyond.

On completion of the study, the statistical end-point gets either a pass or fail. Each phase of development has a new end-point:

- preclinical proof of safety
- clinical proof of safety (Phase I)
- further clinical proof of safety and efficacy (Phases II and III).

Drugs reaching their end-points are met with fanfares and the waving of flags. Press announcements follow, and plans are put into place for the journey to the next end point. Similar celebrations take place if that also succeeds, until that one in 250 reaches approval as a drug for patients.

During this time, the drug developer fixes its eyes firmly on the regulator, with the case report form representing the patient. The case report form records everything that has happened to the patient during the trial for inclusion in the regulatory filing dossier. It can be electronic or paper.

Chapter Seven

The net result is that patients and the many healthcare professionals are not on the radar screen during the development stage as the pharma companies and regulatory authorities do their dance. Let's discuss regulatory authorities when it comes to this gap.

Regulators are getting in the way of the patient-physician interface.

For this point, I need to bring in reinforcements because this is not an area of my work. The expert witness is Dr. Gary Acton. We have worked together on three occasions, at Vanguard Medica circa 2000, Neuropharm circa 2007, and Antisoma circa 2009. As is the silo nature of this industry, we interacted only through the odd nod in the corridor and quick niceties as we changed companies. In work terms, clinical directors and commercial supply chain folk were a million miles apart – intentionally.

Dr. Acton and I have kept in touch over the years and I was delighted to read his book on life in oncology development, *Sympathy for the Devil*. It is beautifully written. We will hear from Dr. Acton again later, but first we need to hear his thoughts on regulation and the clinic.

I offer a word of warning: Dr. Acton does not mince words, which, of course, is a good thing. What follows is his account of how, in the name of keeping patients safe and free from harm, regulators can stifle HCPs ability to make subtle judgements on what is best for their patients.

Q. What do you think of the current patient-physician interface?

A. That is best answered with a recent example of the difficulties and dilemmas we all face when having to deal with recalcitrant regulation, as presented by the extraordinary trans-Atlantic story of the use of Genentech's 'Avastin' in breast cancer which has resulted in greater US-European face-off than at any other time since the American War of Independence of two-and-a-half centuries ago.

Avastin (bevacizumab) is a novel antibody treatment that targets the profuse blood supply upon which tumours depend for their survival, rather than attacking the cancer cells themselves. When combined with conventional chemotherapy, it should therefore provide a double-barreled shotgun blast to predatory malignancies. The drug has proved hugely successful, with a firmly established role in the management of bowel, kidney, brain, lung, ovarian, and cervical cancers, conditions in which it has made a meaningful improvement in the lives of those suffering from these dreadful diseases.

Overall, it is a revolutionary drug. No other biotechnology product has such a wide range of uses. Although it doesn't actually cure anyone of their cancer, it clearly arrests the spread of the disease and buys patients valuable time, something they would otherwise fast be running out of.

However, it is strangely absent, at least in the United States, as a treatment option for breast cancer, one of the most common and devastating of all malignant diagnoses.

Avastin was made available for use in metastatic breast cancer in Europe way back in 2007. The drug continues to be used with benefit in hundreds of thousands of women every year throughout the European community. The approval was on the basis of a single study, (called the E2100 trial), which showed that Avastin, combined with the chemotherapy drug 'paclitaxel', markedly slowed the rate at which the disease progressed. There wasn't really any controversy over it. Certainly nothing like the anguished torment of the debate that was eventually to rage in the United States over whether the drug should be allowed to reach and remain on the market.

The European Medicines Agency has repeatedly reaffirmed its allegiance to the results of E2100, despite the complexities introduced by subsequent North American developments. In December, 2010, the agency's advisory Committee on Human Medicinal Products concluded that: 'Avastin (with paclitaxel)

Chapter Seven

has been convincingly shown to prolong progression-free survival without a negative effect on overall survival.'

In the opinion of the European Medicines Agency itself in February, 2011: 'The results of existing studies on the combination of bevacizumab and paclitaxel are consistent and support a positive effect of therapy with a clear benefit to patients.'

It couldn't be any clearer than that — at least by the opaque standards of a regulator.

In the middle of 2011, the European Medicines Agency had even gone that extra mile and approved Avastin in combination with another chemotherapy drug called 'capecitabine' showing that it was prepared to stand its ground and make a drug that clearly worked as widely available to as many women as possible.

In America, however, the situation could not have been more different. In 2011, Avastin's fate in breast cancer was on the line in the United States despite a total of three Phase III trials supporting its value in treating the disease. The drug was widely used in at least eighty-four countries around the world. But in the United States, it was suddenly fighting for its very existence. Its enemy was none other than the regulators themselves. Patients and clinicians alike looked on in horror as the conflict unfolded. There was a very real possibility that they were about to be deprived of the world's best-selling cancer drug.

Having a drug reach the market is the single dream shared by everyone in biotechnology. Just the possibility of it is enough to counteract the innumerable nightmares caused by all the other drugs that fall by the wayside. But the biggest nightmare of all is the possibility of losing a drug once it has made it through the approval process. The prospect of having a drug withdrawn after it has become comfortably ensconced in the marketplace would cause even the most battle-hardened biotechnology veteran to buckle at the knees.

Once a drug has survived the arduous journey through the development jungle, it ought to be safe and secure when it emerges on the other side. If it hasn't perished along the way, it should be allowed to prosper. But nothing is forever in cancer medicine. Now and then, drugs end up being ejected from the market despite their best attempts. New data can emerge about the safety or efficacy which puts the drugs in a worse light and forces a reappraisal of their viability. It's like having parole revoked and being sent back to prison.

On the rare occasions when this happens, it's the biotechnology equivalent of a natural disaster. Moreover, when it affects the world's biggest biotechnology company and involves its best-selling and most successful cancer drug, it's an earthquake measuring a ten on the Richter scale. The reverberations and aftershocks are felt everywhere. No one and nothing is safe. The ensuing tsunami sweeps away all in front of it.

In the summer of 2010, biotechnology was facing its worst-ever humanitarian crisis. There was a very real prospect that Avastin, one of the most widely used cancer drugs in existence, might lose its position in the marketplace in the United States. The unthinkable looked like it might become the unavoidable, as a 'regulators know best' mind-set become a barrier between physicians and their patients.

It is difficult to accurately convey the scope of this development. If Avastin, the granddaddy of them all, wasn't safe, then absolutely nothing else was either. It represented a threat to the very viability of drug development in cancer. Having reached the face of the gold seam, the mine was in danger of being blown up. Who would want to carry on prospecting when confronted with hazards like that? It was like spending all your life paying off the mortgage and then having the bank repossess your home anyway. In this case, though, the house is worth several billion dollars.

Chapter Seven

If the regulators say, 'Jump,' the industry says, 'How High?'

If we are to believe Dr. Acton, there are concerning issues with the regulatory interface between those developing drugs and the healthcare professionals involved. This relates not only to the regulatory arena.

This is commonly accepted throughout the industry. The regulators are omnipotent. What they say goes. The industry has stopped thinking for itself as it hangs on to regulators' apron strings. To confirm this is Peter Savin, former vice president of Global Quality Assurance at GlaxoSmithKline, now editor of the journal *GMP Review*, and an industry consultant like me.

AN EXPERT WITNESS STATEMENT: PETER SAVIN

Q. What is your view on the industry's lead from the regulators?

A. First, many thanks for the opportunity to contribute to your quest and to comment on one of my biggest concerns for the future of our industry, namely, the ever-increasing levels of mandate and documentation that we face in our daily operations.

I need to say that the industry must grow up. It needs to move away from the child-parent relationship it has allowed to develop with the regulators. Waiting to be told what to do by regulators and the ensuing consultants isn't a good sign of organisational capability or a mature culture. If you doubt the depth of this child-parent dependence, when you next attend a conference with presentations from both regulatory and industry speakers, just take time to notice how the room fills up when the regulatory speakers are on stage and how everyone is listening intently and studiously taking pages of notes. Then compare this to the attendance and attention when the industry speakers are on stage.

Q. I've witnessed that for myself many times. What impact do you think this dependence has had on working practices in the industry?

A. Having worked for forty years in the industry, mostly in manufacturing quality and latterly as a consultant, I've had the opportunity to see the birth of good manufacturing practice and how it has grown and matured. Correspondingly, I've also seen that the biggest and ever-increasing risk that pharmaceutical manufacturing operations face is that of regulatory noncompliance. It saddens me that the public and regulatory perception of our industry and the trust they have in us has plummeted in the past ten years, from being the most ethical industry to being ranked alongside the oil and banking industries. This decline has been caused largely by increasing regulatory censure and the sheer size of fines being imposed on companies through the US legal system. Something needs to be done to reverse this downward trend in our reputation, and we need to address the compliance issue as a first step.

Q. What do you think is at the bottom of this trend?

A. The behaviour of the industry, as it aspires to continually demonstrate compliance in the dynamic and growing regulatory environment, means that already well-controlled companies often try to show they are better than the regulations and implement more procedures, controls, and monitoring than are necessary. In addition, the typical response from companies facing regulatory censure is an explosion of self-imposed policies, procedures, and documentation, often advised by some pharmaceutical consultants that strive to prove their value.

We fail to understand that the consequence of what we are doing is actually worse than zero payback. The almost exponential increase in documentation has ironically been accompanied by a significant increase in regulatory criticism of companies. There is a clear link between procedural non-compliances and complaints, and the increase in documentation.

For some reason, there is a commonly held belief that the best response to regulatory censure is to generate more paperwork. It is sad, but true, that GMP really has come to mean great mountains of paperwork rather than good manufacturing practice. What is also true is that this has not resulted in better-quality products, although in the United States it has enabled huge fines to be extracted from pharma companies. But that is another topic worthy of open discussion.

So the root causes of the problems lie with both the regulators and the industry itself. Both fail to recognise that this continual drive for ever-increasing complexity is not sustainable, and it certainly isn't intelligent. Remember the saying: 'Any intelligent fool can make things bigger and more complex. It takes a touch of genius and a lot of courage to move in the opposite direction.' It is time for the foolishness of unnecessary complexity to stop and courage to be demonstrated throughout the industry.

There is serious work to be done, then, to rectify this debilitating relationship problem.

Now we move on to the effects of advanced therapies and diagnostics on the industry.

Patient markets are shrinking irreversibly

The size of markets for pharma products is shrinking with the realisation that many drugs help only a certain proportion of those on clinical trials, not the entire population for the disease state. With the emergence of genetic testing and more powerful diagnosis, we are likely to find approved drugs applying to much smaller patient groups, thus reducing the sales revenue, unless the industry increases prices.

What we have learned of stratified and personalised medicine is going to make this even more extreme and force companies to think more carefully and deeply about the patients they serve. The question arises as to whether pharma companies will be able to operate over so many diverse disease areas. The emergence of stratified medicine is set to demand ever-deepening knowledge-banks of people's biological characteristics with respect to particular diseased states. The critical mass required to build these knowledge bases is likely to severely restrict coverage across multiple therapeutic areas.

Pharma marketing has lost its way

Pharma spends significant time, effort and mountains of cash on marketing their product portfolios. Is that really money and effort well-directed?

To help us with this topic, we turn to our expert witness, Dr. Graham Cox, MD, co-founder and co-inventor at SHOFT, (a novel device to reduce car seat-belt back pain). Graham is a former senior marketing executive at Astra Zenica. After a few chats on Skype, I realised Graham was not the typical pharma senior marketing executive. He was firmly rooted in the reality of what is going wrong and active in plotting a path for the future.

This is what he has to say on the subject:

Q. What's the problem with marketing in pharma?

A. Before I answer that, let's get back to basics. Making products that do things, telling people about them and selling them is a process that has been going on for many thousands of years. However, it might have been the great industrial revolution that led to a more formal recognition of what we might call 'Marketing 1.0', which was 'tell people about your product and some buy it'. Maybe this was the age of advertising where the bigger the spend and the more creative the advert, the more the company sold. A huge over-simplification, but I hope you'll agree things were a bit more straightforward then.

Chapter Seven

Then in the 1970s and 80s, the market research industry gained momentum to give rise to 'Marketing 2.0'. This new marketing model was based on the seemingly obvious truth that 'if you find out what people want, then go and make it, there will be a market ready and waiting for your product/service'. The sophistication, or should I say complexity, of the market research machine in driving decision-making has become so engrained into our thinking that, for many, it would be foolish to make anything - a concept, a product etc. - without involving in-depth market research every step of the way.

The deep insights in 'Marketing 3.0' are attributed to marketing guru Philip Kotler, where marketing focuses on the customer as a human being in its entirety with material, emotional and spiritual needs, a process capable of satisfying humanism's noblest instances. Kotler asserts: 'Those companies that will adopt Marketing 3.0 will have an edge because they will be able to combine a quality product/service with a mission imbued with positive values. Essentially, Marketing 3.0 is a mix of cultural, spiritual, and collaborative marketing .

Most non-pharma companies have moved on to Marketing 3.0, but pharma still supports departments and an industry that churns out data that has never been proven to help in decision-making.

Q. Why do you think pharma has been left behind?

A. Pharma is a very conservative business and getting change takes a long time. Here's an example: using Marketing 2.0 thinking, Pharma regularly spends huge sums of money on 'conjoint' analyses, (from $650K to well over $1M). These are pieces of market research that claim to measure customer preference structures. Companies feed in potential promotional claims for the drug and, using clever software algorithms, the conjoint 'black box' spews out preference share for combinations of claims. It sounds too good to be true, and indeed it is. Although it's easy to see how any company

would like to know how many sales they can attach to a set of claims, pretty much all of this has been proven to be no more accurate than much smaller and zero cost internal conjoints, (Satter and Hensel-Börner, In Conjoint Measurement: Methods and Applications: 2000, Springer Verlag, Berlin, p121-133).
In addition, psychological tests have shown quite clearly that what people say they might do - preference share - has little bearing on what they actually do - market share and sales.
As other industries move on, pharma is left with historic templated budgets that need to be spent, (or it will be lost next year and look 'odd' against other drug budgets in the pipeline). So rather than review the value of these expensive exercises, they continue to hide behind them, blindly making decisions on flawed methodology.

Q. So is pharma wasting money on unproven market research?

A. Indeed. Marketing continues to have huge, unquestioned budgets to hold think-tanks, panel discussions and the obligatory advisory boards. Although asking customers what they want all sounds logical, most of this is a total waste of money.
Yet pharma seem trapped holding a perception where they feel naked without having this largely consensus-driven information to convince the company the drug is on the right track. The market research industry feeds off this lack of confidence and promises better decision-making, but delivers 'accurately wrong' rather than 'roughly right' results. With only one in four launched drugs ever repaying its R&D cost, the logic and justification for this huge market research spend just doesn't hold.

Q. So it's really just 'bad science'?

A. Ironic, isn't it? But, yes. I would say, though, that great marketing is a blend of pressure-testing prototype ideas and taking bold decisions. Many have read about huge marketing blunders where the logic seems straightforward but the product didn't sell. A lot of the reasons for failure are in the methodology of the market research. If you take advertising slogans or messages, these are traditionally tested with customers, sometimes across many countries. The intention is to get a set of messages that resonate with the customer. However, many market research agencies tend to aggregate responses so the client gets to choose the messages that 'on average' the sample customers liked.

Unfortunately, creating a successful product isn't like that. Polarising customer views is what creates success. Take Rolex, Porsche, Apple, etc.. Although highly successful, it's easy to find people who really dislike what each stands for... and that's the crux of it. A pharma brand needs to stand for something, but most products end up right in the graveyard of 'average' because they avoid clear polarising messages and instead plump for the 'safe' middle ground. The conservative scientific thinking of pharma always like to be in the safe zone, although it's far from safe when looking at the resultant sales.

Much food for thought here, and more to follow.

New business models are sitting on a knife edge

This next reality is based on Big Pharma being the alpha male of the industry. Biotech and Virtual Pharma need to make deals with the large pharma companies to survive. Companies in generics and biosimilars depend on Big Pharma to get the original patented products onto the market. The huge contractor base would fall apart if it could not build business plans on work coming from the Big Pharma world, and wholesalers would have no products to buy and sell without Big Pharma loading the pipeline.

If we continue on the current trajectory, there is every chance that the industry will fall like a house of cards.

Governments pouring money into science won't help

All the scientific grant funding and various other supporting financial initiatives on governmental menus globally will be to no avail unless the issues we discuss above are addressed at a fundamental level. More of the same will not cut the mustard.

Here, in the UK, we are bombarded almost daily with multi-million pound funding calls to solve this or that particular scientific conundrum. It is similar across the European landscape, and no doubt the same in most other countries across the globe, as they to seek to capitalise on future opportunities in 21st century healthcare.

Hopefully, readers will have gleaned that availability of funds is much less of an issue than finding the individuals and companies that are able to translate science into workable solutions for patients and healthcare professionals, often with extremely modest budgets.

Universities and colleges have caught the science bug

Using no science whatsoever, I did a web-search on university courses in pharmaceuticals and biopharmaceuticals. Below is the resulting summary I was able to piece together by randomly selecting from the content of courses on offer. Hopefully the following is indicative of the issue we face.

BSc in Pharmaceuticals/Pharmaceutics

First year

- Compounding
- Formulation Chemistry
- Pharmaceutical Processes and Technologies
- Basic Microbiology

- Professional and Quantitative Science Skills
- Cell Biology and Biochemistry

Second year
- Product Formulation
- Chemical Analysis, Quality and Stability
- Applied Pharmacology
- Pharmaceutical Microbiology
- Product Formulation

Third year
- Quality Assurance and Quality by Design Principles
- Project
- Development and Manufacture of Pharmaceutical Products
- Pharmaceutical Materials Science

MSc in Pharmaceuticals/Biopharmaceuticals
- Dosage Forms and PCkinetics
- Delivering Gene and Therapeutic Proteins
- Essential Research and Study Skills
- Research Manipulation
- Pharmaceutical Nanotechnology
- Gene Cloning, Expression and Analysis
- Bioinformatics
- Entrepreneurship and Innovation
- Research Project

These are of course essential skills for those embarking and moving onward with careers in the pharmaceutical and biopharmaceutical industry. Note, however, the absence of translational skills to accompany these skills, and also the lack of focus on end-products. The only mention of manufacture in the BSc programme is in the third year of study; and for the MSc, it doesn't even make the starting grid.

The harsh reality is that universities and colleges are setting and reinforcing a reductionist-thinking mentality that stays with its offspring for life. Schools of learning will do well to think long and hard on that.

8 : IT'S THE SYSTEM WOT DONE IT, YOUR HONOUR

A shameful admission before we go on

At this crucial point, I need to make a shameful yet cathartic admission from my past working life: I used to carry a clipboard, stopwatch attached, timing folk as they went about their daily tasks. Even worse, I would rate the speed at which they worked against a scale, and then tell them how many widgets they had to produce that day, and every other day, until management told them to stop, or they left to find another, more satisfying job.

The system had given people like me titles, variously termed 'work study officer', 'time and motion guy' and 'industrial engineer' (IE). I liked to call myself an IE, but the workers preferred less complimentary titles often containing expletives for deletion before public consumption.

We were not a popular breed and were regarded as a tool of management, which indeed we were. The reason why I mention this is because that discipline grew into the foundation for Japan's transformational work in the 1950s and 1960s, starting in the auto industry with the likes of Toyota, Honda and Nissan, and spreading to other sectors quite quickly.

They managed it because they took industrial engineering's powerful tools for studying systems of work of out of the hands of management (and me!) and gave them to the workers. Those workers had a purpose – to make Japan strong again following the ravages of the World War II.

Western experts, such as Walter A. Shewhart, W. Edwards Deming, et al, taught the skills of statistical quality control, problem-solving and other IE techniques required to develop and make high quality products without the equivalent high costs. In fact, the opposite happened – costs tumbled. The rest, as they say, is history.

The reason why this is important is because these people and companies developed a whole new, systems-based approach to the business of producing products and services for demanding customer markets. They were christened 'production systems', the most well-known being the Toyota Production System, or TPS for short.

It is beyond the scope of this book to delve into the secret of their success, albeit it is on the agenda for another book to follow.

It will suffice for now to recognise the vital part systems-thinking will have to play in any transformation for the pharma industry. So, let's talk about it.

ENTER SOCIO-TECHNICAL SYSTEMS

With the messy stuff behind us, it's time to rise above the specifics of an industry in crisis to enter a world we all share – Socio-Technical Systems – be they in healthcare, government, education, industry, or just you, chilling out at home, streaming your favourite film on Netflix.

It is vitally important to move to this higher level as the medicines industry appears to have carved out a position in the industrial world where it is regarded as 'different' to any other sector. In doing that, it has managed to excuse itself from the necessary underpinning hard-yards required to successfully bring innovative products to market.

In order to explain the folly in this, we need sound, defensible principles as proof, taken from those who know and have done it better.

Chapter Eight

Complex theories abound in the realms of socio-technical systems theory and a multitude of different approaches have been advanced over the years. Here we will keep it simple and focussed exclusively on 'just enough' theory, and plenty of practice, to achieve the aim of finding and detailing a new improved path for PCs and the medicines industry. Whilst we will draw on an eclectic mix of 'whole systems' expertise, our steely focus will fix onto the socio-technical systems dear to our hearts in this book - those making and supplying products and services to commercial markets.

If you are mildly perturbed by the word 'theory', rest easy. This treatment of socio-technical systems will be practical and grounded; and there is a government health warning to stalwarts of academic rigour arriving here by accident or design. What follows is based on personal experience and life-long learning, none of it written up in papers based on research best practice. Oh, and there are a few giants from the world of business thrown in for good measure.

I've drawn heavily on the disciplines of production and industrial engineering. I studied and was trained in both, and they are the foundation stones of modern socio-technical systems design and improvement, especially in relation to the Japanese automotive revolution. We will draw on my Executive MBA at Cranfield School of Management which has been a magnificent resource to have stashed in my back pocket.

WHAT IS A SOCIO-TECHNICAL SYSTEM?

Socio-technical systems, (a term coined by Eric Trist, Ken Bamforth and Fred Emery in the World War II era, based on their work in English coal mines at the Tavistock Institute in London), exist when people band together with a purposeful end in mind. The 'technical' component reflects the human ingenious predisposition to use non-human elements, such as machinery, equipment and technologies, as levers in support of these ends.

A definition of 'technical' as taken from the Oxford Dictionary is: 'involving or concerned with applied and industrial sciences.' The terms underlined are crucial because they have become noticeably absent from the medicines industry of today.

Now we turn to a body of thinking attributed to Russell Ackoff, as outlined in the book, *Systems Thinking for Curious Managers*. Ackoff was a prolific writer on systems and systems thinking and he mentored many an expert in the field. One of them, Bill Bellows, is quoted in the book and it is his definition we see below, simple, straightforward and to the point, just the way we like it:

'A [socio-technical] system is a set or pattern of relationships that work together in some fashion. [Socio-technical] systems can accomplish things that would be impossible if the same elements were put into random relationships, or no relationships at all.'

Bill goes on to say: *'Although we may sometimes take it for granted, we get enormous value from [socio-technical] systems every day. We benefit continually from various smart puttings-together of resources that provide us with food, transportation, education, goods and services.'*

Bill is now deputy director of the W. Edwards Deming Institute, continuing with his inspirational work in the world of industrial systems design and improvement, helping deliver all those benefits he talks about above.

A SPORTING ANALOGY

To help our understanding, we will start with a sporting analogy hopefully not patronising to those accomplished systems thinkers among us.

Let's consider regulars at our local pub joining a Sunday morning football league. They are in it for fun and enjoyment, with a little bit of fitness thrown in. The guys chip in for meals, transport and other out-of-pocket expenses, whilst never losing sight of the customary hours spent in the bar and those important social relationships involved.

Suppose they have some success and they decide to join a more competitive Saturday afternoon football league. Their purpose will now have changed, looking towards moving up the league rankings, winning matches, getting a few awards and even a cup or two; maybe recognition from friends and family too.

Their system will now have to adapt as they spend less time drinking at the bar and more on the training ground. The rules of engagement need to change as the impact of not turning up for a game or turning in a poor performance are magnified. Fundamentally, the changed purpose calls for changes in actions and behaviour – system outputs.

After topping the amateur leagues, they decide to join a professional football league, getting paid for the privilege of playing. Now they spend no time in the bar and every working hour in training. Their new-found purpose is to earn a living from the system. Imagine again how rules, actions and behaviour must change as the consequences of not meeting the purpose escalate.

SOME PRACTICAL EXAMPLES FROM BUSINESS AND SPORT

We promised some giants of business would lend a hand, and we start with Steve Jobs of Apple fame. Below is an extract from a video of his where I managed to jot down his musings:

'These are the keys to Apple:

We are an incredibly collaborative company.

Do you know how many committees we have at Apple? – Zero

We are organised like a start-up:

1 person in charge of iPhone OS software.

1 person in charge of MAC hardware.

1 person in charge of iPhone hardware engineering

1 person in charge of w/w marketing.

1 person in charge of operations.

We are the biggest start-up on the planet.

And we all meet for three hours once a week and we talk about everything we are doing, the whole business.

And there's tremendous teamwork at the top of the company which filters down to tremendous teamwork throughout the company.

And teamwork is dependent on trusting the other folks to come through with their part without watching them all the time.

Trusting that they are going to come through with their part – and that's what we do really well, we are great at figuring out how to divide things up into these great teams that we have. We all work on the same things and touch bases frequently and bring it all together into a product.

We do that really well and so what I do all day is meet with teams of people.

And work on ideas and solve problems to make new products and make new marketing programmes. Whatever it is.'

Spot on, Steve. Armed with those principles, it is no coincidence that Steve Jobs achieved what he did.

You may have been able to relate some of this to your own experiences of getting things done in complex systems. Feel free

Chapter Eight

to continue doing that, because in this example, and those to follow here, there are common, foundational principles which we will draw out in later conclusions.

Next up is Jeff Bezos of Amazon.

I don't need to research anything on Jeff Bezos - the proof is in his puddings. I've heard he worked for many years before making any profit, and that the work was long, demanding, and involved growing teams of people working on incredibly novel service offerings. He's also now, of course, the richest man in the world.

Media reports that flash up on the screen sometimes talk about Amazon operating sweatshops and not treating its workers particularly well. Who knows if that is true or not? The thing is, though, generally, that if quality stuff comes out of a system, there are normally good things happening inside.

My experience of Amazon has been of quality delivered consistently, with the occasional hiccup that gets corrected PDQ. The overriding experience is one of trust. Amazon trusts that if I complain about my delivery, I'm not trying to pull one over on them. They'll send me another if I say its faulty and not even ask for the original back as proof, very often.

Even with a more complex service offering, such as self-publishing a book, their focus on the end-user is extraordinary. (It's been me a few times, through CreateSpace and KDP). They are right there with you every step of the way.

Next to enter the stage is the Welsh rugby team and its massively understated coach, Warren Gatland.

As a passionate Welshman, it would be remiss of me not to include our wonderful team. This socio-technical system, especially given the size of Wales, has performed remarkably well over the years, consistently producing world class talent and stunning outcomes. As a passionate Welshman, please forgive me if I whisper in your ear: 'Warren is a Kiwi'. Keep that to yourself.

His achievements with Wales have been nothing less than spectacular. His understated style, however, belies his skill and ingenuity in building such a high performing socio-technical system. You only need to watch his back-office team on match day beavering away at the analytics, tactical adjustments and the million other things needed to support those on the field of play.

Those on the field have been drilled to within an inch of their lives. Nothing is left to chance, every eventuality catered for.

On the bench sit reinforcements, (not also-rans there to make up the numbers). with a pre-determined role to play as the match unfolds, and the subs are called on depending on how things are turning out. They are happy bunnies, secure in the knowledge they are an integral part of proceedings.

That's the visible bit. Like all good icebergs, most of it is below water. Or maybe a closer analogy is a tree, where the roots go down to collect the food and water needed to grow big and strong above ground. Warren and his supporting team's work with the Welsh regional network of clubs has been heroic, resulting in ever-increasing strength in depth and fierce competition for those cherished places on the field.

Having kept the secret of Warren's origins, it should be safe to mention he was born to this way of working having grown up in probably the world's highest performing sporting socio-technical system: the New Zealand All-Blacks. In his excellent book, *Legacy*, James Kerr shares the secrets of that team's success. It's a master text in organisational culture and leadership. You didn't hear that from me, right?

Chapter Eight

Let's now finish the practical stuff with an excursion into another example of systems thinkers in action.

In 2011, I received an email from the well-known UK entrepreneur, Kavita Oberoi OBE. She told me she shared a charitable committee with the COO of UPS's international arm who wanted someone to facilitate two roundtables, in Paris and Rome, for their healthcare clients. To cut a long tale short, she engaged me as a consultant and that is where I met Dan Gagnon, then UPS EU Healthcare marketing and strategy director, based in Brussels.

Subsequently we worked on a few other projects related to homecare logistics, presenting at UPS's annual conference in Budapest, 2014, and helping with a pre-wholesaler acquisition in Italy.

In working with Dan, I learned a lot about the strength of the UPS culture:

- Most individuals in management started as a sorter, loader, or driver on the front line and moved up the ranks.

- An industrial engineering (systems) mind-set permeated the entire organisation whose mantra is: To be constructively dissatisfied'.

- The notion 'you get what you measure' is especially important in delivering to end-user expectations through customer service measures.

- Mutually supportive relationships, collaboration, and knowledge sharing.

- Immense pride in being a UPS-er.

- Long, rewarding careers for so many of its employees.

Roughly about the time I first hooked up with Dan, UPS was awarded the contract to handle the logistics for the UK's Olympic

Games, to be held in 2012. Here was the potential to become famous for all the wrong reasons – logistics is not easy at the best of times, even if only sending a small package to a long-lost cousin four thousand miles away in a remote village somewhere in the back of beyond. This was going to be one of the most complex logistical challenges the world had ever known.

When Dan told me they had all 'holed-up' in a rented nerve-centre in the heart of London, specifically to stay aligned and focused on the task ahead, I thought to myself: 'yes, systems thinking in action again, they'll nail this'…And they did!

NOW FOR SOME ACADEMIC RIGOUR TO ADD TO THE MIX

We doubt if the protagonists in the above had studied systems thinking, yet they were experts at it.

Another in that mould, in my humble opinion, is Professor Michael Porter. For those not familiar with the professor's global profile in business and competitive strategy, he is an economist, researcher, author, advisor, speaker and teacher at Harvard Business School. His teachings are prolific, insightful and incredibly novel. I'm sure he won't be overly flattered to be included here – he is much sought after in business circles where systems thinking doesn't get much air-time – but hopefully he will recognise the connections we make with his work.

We will focus on the Professor's 'Value Chain Model' very well known in the world of business strategy. (Some of this material may seem a bit heavier than what we have been used to so far, but please try to stay with it as far as you can; hopefully it will bear fruit as we get towards the end.)

I first referenced the Professor's model in my 2011 book, *Supply Chain Management In The Drug Industry: Delivering Patient Value*

Chapter Eight

for Pharmaceuticals and Biologics. I continue to include this seminal work in my presentations today. It seems ironic to me that this is probably one of *the* most instructional books on strategic supply chain management ever written – without any direct mention of this specialist subject!

The model describes how each firm engages in multiple activities to create value which ultimately must be greater than the cost of those activities. Firms along the value chain will generate a profit margin, then, to allow them to survive and grow, the underpinning equation being:

Value Created (VC) - Cost to Deliver (CD) = Gross Profit (GP)

VC is nothing other than the money customers are willing to pay for your product or service – it is a 'sharp end' measure. No amount of alleged VC can be claimed unless a paying customer is willing to shell out for it. So often, firms get this wrong because they use internal perspectives to measure VC.

Similarly, cost is the hard measure of cash outflow when running a business. We need to be ever-vigilant that we do not record cost savings in the business that are merely moving from one pocket to another and should thus not be used to justify investment opportunities.

VC and CD must move in opposing directions to consistently maintain competitive advantage. Rather a simple notion, don't you think? In practice, of course, a touch more challenging.

The model categorises any firm's activities into two types: primary and support. Neither is classed as more important relative to the other. It also distinguishes activities directly involved in creating sales and delivering to customers from those activities necessary to move VC and CD in the opposing directions we mentioned earlier. Both sets of activities have the potential to create competitive advantage.

The diagram below depicts the model:

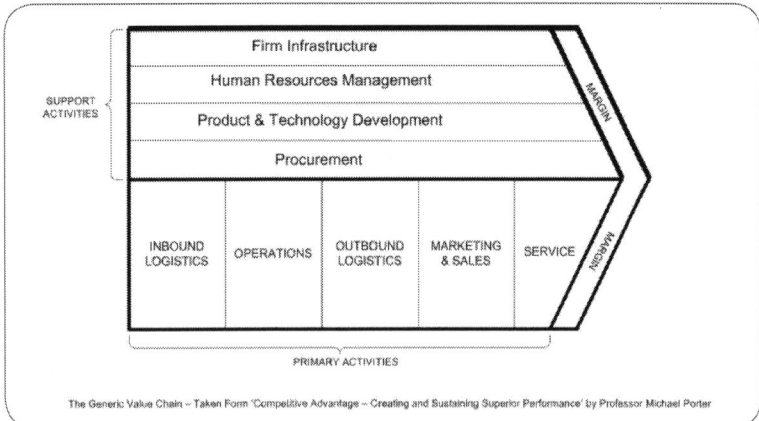

The main elements of the model can be summarised as follows:

Primary activities - these are all the activities required to produce, deliver, sell and service the final product:

- Inbound logistics - activities associated with receiving, storing and making available all the inputs required for operations.

- Operations - activities necessary to transform inputs into outputs. These will include operations such machining, blending, filtering, freeze drying, packaging, testing etc..

- Outbound logistics - these are activities such as transporting, warehousing, and sales order processing.

- Marketing and sales - activities focussed on providing a means for purchasers to buy products and providing a stimulus to purchase.

- After sales service - including provision of service and spare parts, installation and customer training.

- Support activities - these are defined as activities that support the primary activities and help differentiate the offering. They are categorised under the following headings:

- Firm infrastructure – these activities are defined as supporting the firm, rather than individual activities. Included are general management, finance and accounting, information systems etc.. Porter uses the example of a telephone operating company gaining significant competitive advantage by maintaining effective relationships with regulatory bodies.

- Human resources – activities such as recruiting, training, motivating and rewarding staff are included. Competitive advantage can be gained here by attracting talent and developing critical skill-sets that are needed.

- Product and technology development. The definition of technology covers developments that can impact either VC and CD, or both. This area is receiving unprecedented attention in medicine these days. Many will be fully aware of this as the digital economy takes hold and artificial intelligence (AI) and machine learning (ML) are perceived as great opportunity areas.

- Procurement – the purchase of input materials to the business. It includes primary inputs such as raw materials, machinery and equipment, production consumables, for example, plus support areas such as laboratory and office supplies, computer hardware and consultancy services. An important point made is that procurement occurs across the business and does not always receive due attention from those involved. The text makes the case for improved procurement practices to strongly affect cost, quality and other important business benefits.

The model states that competitive advantage can be enhanced through effective linkages. The professor explains linkages as: 'the relationship between the way one value activity is performed, and the cost or performance of another'.

To illustrate, if those undertaking the procurement process for the firm secure above average quality materials for production, then there may be an important reduction in down-time and waste on the factory floor. This would have a positive impact on both VC and CD.

The professor defines two types of linkage:

- Those within the value chain of the firm – internal linkages.
- Those between upstream and downstream firms – vertical linkages.

Linkages can be:

- Primary-Primary
- Primary-Secondary
- Secondary-Secondary

Why is that this all so important? It is because the physical supply (value) chain is the vehicle by which customers get their products and services, and the VC and CD are an accumulation of all that joining up of linkages along the way. As these linkages are properly and increasingly meshed together, so too does competitive advantage increase, and business or sporting success ensues – as naturally as day follows night.

LEARNING FROM DISASTER TOO

That's it from the world of giants, and what a feast of learning we found there, to be revisited and recapped later.

We now move on to the opposite end of spectrum, the (moral) dwarves and dunces of the socio-technical systems world. There will be an equal amount of learning here too because in errors and mistakes lie valuable opportunities to discover better ways of working. We begin with the UK political system and the decision to put forward proposals in 2010 to move to a fixed-term parliament.

A POLITICAL LOG-JAM ENSUES

The Fixed-term Parliament Act 2011 was passed during a Conservative-Liberal Democrat coalition government. The coalition aspect itself should have been a warning bell. The various intricacies of political maneuverings are amplified several-fold when two very ideologically different parties try to work together in a power sharing arrangement. Add to that that the coalition was a rather one-sided affair in the power stakes and the seeds of demise were all but sown.

So the decision to change the parliamentary rules was made, passed and implemented, for better or for worse. I am not the best person to go into all the details. There are others far more qualified to do so, and anyway, the low-down will be there for all to find with the help of your friendly internet search-engine. We will focus here on the (unintended?) consequence of the rule change.

With it now virtually impossible to oust a government before its five years are up, the incumbent government is given licence to thumb its nose at calls to stand down, no matter how extreme its incompetence happens to be. Wishing to avoid the slings and arrows of the raging Brexit debate and trying to stay on neutral ground for the sake of holding your attention, it would be hard to conclude that the fixed term idea has been a success for our country. Parliament is currently in deadlock and has been so, in various guises, for coming up to three years now.

A high-level assessment of the outcome might suggest that the darker side of human nature has presided as politicians try to hang onto their seats for as long as they possibly can and warring factions in both parties knock lumps out of each other in the absence of the once readily available remedy: to force a government to stand down and move over before the cliff edge appears.

Our next example, this time a life or death one, relates to the supply and pricing of modern-day insulin, especially as it applies to US.

INSULIN HEROES, SUBSUMED BY DUNCES

In 1921, on a shoestring budget at the University of Toronto, several young scientists began investigating a possible treatment for Type 1 diabetes. They found that by grinding up and purifying animal pancreases and then regularly injecting the material, they could treat Type 1 diabetes in dogs.

After first testing the drug for safety by injecting themselves, the scientists treated a 14-year-old boy with Type 1 diabetes. His recovery was almost miraculous, going from death's door to good health in a matter of weeks.

By 1923, the scientists had won the Nobel prize and the treatment had entered mass production in collaboration with Eli Lilly and Company and the Swedish organisation Nordisk. The scientists patented the drug and sold it to the University of Toronto for three dollar, (one dollar for each researcher), thinking that this was the best way to ensure that affordable treatment would be available to everyone who needed it.

With a fast forward to the future, fast-acting 'analog' insulins were pioneered with Lilly's 'HumaLog' in 1996, but when Novo Nordisk entered the market four years later with its own analog insulin, 'NovoLog' prices did not decrease due to competition. Instead, Lilly and Nordisk followed each other closely in an exponential price increase. When HumaLog was first introduced, it cost $21. At the time of writing, HumaLog costs [$295.35] per

Chapter Eight

vial and NovoLog costs [$296.27]. The older 'human' insulins like 'Humalin' are less expensive, but far less effective in treating Type 1 diabetes — yet even these primitive insulins have increased dramatically in price since their introduction in 1982.

The HPR article 'How Insulin Became Unaffordable' recounted the tragic case of Alec Raeshawn Smith whose body stopped producing insulin when he was 24 – he had become a Type 1 diabetic. The article goes on: 'For two years, Smith managed his condition relatively well. But it wasn't easy financially. On May 20, 2017, Smith turned 26, ageing out of his parents' insurance.' He didn't qualify for government assistance with his insulin payments, and when he went to pick up his insulin in early June, the bill was over $1300 without insurance. He couldn't afford the medicine that day and decided to ration his remaining insulin until he was paid. He didn't tell his family.

On June 25, Smith went to dinner with his girlfriend where he complained about stomach pains. It was the last time anyone saw him alive. He called in sick to work the next day. On June 27, Smith was found dead in his apartment. RIP Alec Raeshawn Smith. Our hearts go out to his mother, Nicole Smith-Holt, his family, and all those who knew and loved him.

Impossible not to shed a tear over this sickening tragedy, nor wonder how the executive boards within those companies sleep at night.

Socio-technical systems can be cruel and heartless.

Returning to these eye-watering prices, we hear the voice of David Nathan, a professor at Harvard Medical School, in an interview with the HPR. 'There hasn't been a molecule changed in them. There hasn't been a bit of change in terms of their synthesis, their manufacturing, and yet the costs have gone up extraordinarily. There are no adults in the room to tell the companies they can't charge whatever they feel like.'

Readers may ponder on what those three worthy scientists from way back would be thinking now, having sold the patent to the original insulin for just $3 and risked their lives in developing the medical breakthrough.

THE DISASTER THAT NEVER HAPPENED: HOW 'NO PATENT' SAVED THOUSANDS OF CHILDREN FROM SUFFERING

The first effective polio vaccine was developed in 1952 by Jonas Salk and a team at the University of Pittsburgh. Salk went on CBS radio to report a successful test on a small group of adults and children on 26 March, 1953; two days later the results were published.

Beginning 23 February, 1954, the vaccine was tested at Arsenal Elementary School and the Watson Home for Children in Pittsburgh, Pennsylvania.

On April 12, 1955, Edward R. Murrow asked Jonas Salk who owned the patent to the polio vaccine. 'Well, the people, I would say,' Salk responded. 'There is no patent. Could you patent the sun?'

By the time of his chat with Murrow, which aired on the day the polio vaccine was announced as safe and 90 percent effective, Salk was already more messiah than virologist to the average American. Polio paralysed between 13,000 and 20,000 children annually in the last pre-vaccine years, and Salk was the face of the inoculation initiative. Appearing on television to present the vaccine as a gift to the American people was a public relations masterstroke.

One critic of Big Pharma called Salk 'the foster parent of children around the world, with no thought of the money he could make by withholding the vaccine from the children of the poor'.

Whatever happened to the system that produced such selfless individuals as we hear of above? The practice of withholding medicines from patients until the ransom is paid is now endemic throughout the industry, and it's getting worse.

In the search for answers, we re-name Socio-Technical Systems as 'People-Purpose Systems', PPS for short, and sort out some principles under that heading to stand us in good stead for our challenge ahead.

9 : THE PEOPLE-PURPOSE SYSTEM (PPS) STEPS IN TO HELP

WHY DO WE NEED TO KNOW ABOUT PPS?

You don't need to know about PPS if you have no interest in ever achieving anything in your life. If that is you, don't just skip this chapter, ditch the book – it'll do nothing for you.

If, however, you want to have a purpose in life, with a means to deliver on that, this chapter is for you. It does not attempt to provide a rigorous model of academic systems thinking. The main idea is to give us enough understanding to achieve our purpose here – radical and sustainable transformation of the medicines industry. That can't be too difficult, can it?

Remember that the following relates to a PPS in the business of delivering products and services destined to end-user markets.

THE FUNDAMENTALS

As we go through the fundamentals, feel free to refer to the previous chapter looking for evidence that we are on the right track. The giants will provide support for the right things to do, and the moral dwarfs and dunces the converse.

Beginning with the PPS itself, if we take an example from my own experience, that may help.

In writing this book, I've got a PPS on the go. There are numerous people working with me in all kinds of ways, mainly unpaid, until we get it out there. We are, and will continue to be, using available non-human resources as levers in many areas.

The purpose of our PPS is to create a resource that provides knowledge to help catalyse radical change for the better in the medicines industry. We will know that's been achieved when said resource pops out of the PPS onto shelves – the output.

A PPS must have at least one purposeful end in mind and an output, or possibly multiple outputs, that deliver on the purpose. We may produce a paperback, webinar, podcast, or eBook. All contribute to the purpose. So far, so good.

The output can't just be approximate to what's needed– it must do the business for those we are trying to influence. To do that, we must walk a mile in their shoes. In fact, we should surprise them with a brand-new pair of shoes beyond their wildest dreams. If that means walking 1,000, 10,000 or millions of miles in their footwear, then so be it.

Once our book has walked as many miles as is needed, we must then find ingenious ways to organise ourselves to deliver on our promise of a vehicle for transformational change. Since you are reading this now, we have evidence of a successful PPS in action.

The giants we have talked about are all masters at this. When it happens, end-users are drawn in and well-deserved returns are made. (NB, we adopt the term end-users, rather than customers, as it is the end-user's desire to acquire that creates demand for your offering. Customers often include non-users, only there through the wants of others. Grandparents and sweets spring to mind).

So, we have it then, the fundamentals:

Fundamental No. 1 – A PPS must know end-users of its products and services better than they know themselves.

Giant Jeff Bezos's PPS sheds light on this. The learning to be taken from Amazon here is not mentioned in the earlier chapter,

Chapter Nine

so I shall mention it now. My second book was self-published through Amazon CreateSpace. I had become disenchanted with the traditional publishing model, which is heavily biased towards benefits going into publishers' coffers.

In my case, with the first book, and, I suspect, unless your name is J. K. Rowling, this applies typically, royalties are paid twice a year with a two-month delay after period end. All manner of discounts and rebates are taken out of the list price, and the royalty is a less- than-fabulous ten percent of the net figure.

I joke to people sometimes that I spend more on printer ink cartridges than I earn in royalties. Hang on, that's not a joke, it's fact. Well... almost!

There is little or no marketing effort put behind the book, other than listing in the catalogue and placement on various bookseller websites. Sales reports are updated at the end of each month with no real-time access to the details; you must wait until a few days after month-end. How dare they ask for anything more?

Compare this with Amazon CreateSpace, (and I've done the same with Amazon Kindle).

Royalties are paid within a few days of the end of every month, straight into the bank account, with email confirmation. The reporting system over the month tells you almost instantly, (within a minute or two, believe me – I've bought copies of my own books to prove it), when someone makes a purchase and their country location.

In creating the manuscript and supporting materials, help is on hand readily, if needed.

While there is some artificial intelligence involved, there is also easy access to a real human being. Yes, you heard right, a *real* human being.

So, what do we take from this? Intense attention to the detail of the customer, (end-user from now on), experience is the secret of success. The ability to stay seamlessly connected with your end-user, knowing them better than they know themselves, is what matters; then, being able to join up and engage all the resources required to deliver that experience consistently and predictably, except for the odd hiccup that is sorted quickly when it happens very occasionally.

This is how Jeff Bezos and Amazon can disrupt industries it chooses to enter. It has the potential to do that in finished product sale and distribution of medicines, too, an activity it is actively engaged in.

To do that with the development and production of medicines however, Mr. Bezos et al would need to read our books - and who's to say they won't.

Fundamental No. 2 - A PPS must know its own inner workings and the inter-dependencies of its insides while maintaining a steely focus on the needs and wants of end-users.

Steve Jobs explained that: 'We all meet for three hours once a week and we talk about everything we are doing, the whole business' and 'We all work on the same things and touch bases frequently and bring it all together into a product'.

Professor Porter details it with his insights on linkages, emphasising the crucial importance of different activity areas of the business creating advantage for each other.

Fundamental No. 3 - Understand the concept of 'knock-on' effects, (KOEs), and their potential to have impact inside and outside the PPS.

Sometimes termed the 'The Domino Effect', the notion is that when people and things are joined together, often in ways that are difficult to work out, even the most apparently simple action

Chapter Nine

can result in totally unexpected outcomes. Also, action leads to reaction - important to know when considering strategies to battle competition.

Warren Gatland doesn't shout it from the rooftops, not even from a seat in his back garden, but he knows the importance of getting to the roots that feed the PPS's growth and development in achieving the purpose and desired outputs; understanding the KOEs, (for Welsh rugby fans, no pun intended for the knock on!), required underground that will eventually work its way to the top.

Warren teaches us that stellar performances on the field have their roots years earlier, when little Dafydd was introduced to the game and coached in a supportive and sensitive, (not too sensitive, it is rugby after all), fashion.

He understands that not only simple, unintended actions can lead to chaos, but also that well thought out long-term plans to draw results up from the roots can bear stunningly succulent fruit.

The UPS example is unsurprisingly more of the same, and maybe readers are beginning to see a pattern emerging here? Again, we hear of focus on long-term sustainability of the business based on pride in work and achievements, supportive relationships, joined-up thinking, rewarding career paths, and succession planning throughout. That can only be down to generations of successful and enduring leadership teams at UPS.

Fundamental No. 4 - No man or woman is an island. Build a deep and constantly updated relationship with the world outside and the KOEs involved.

If you think it's complicated inside the PPS, what must it be like on the outside where you have little or no control over matters? For example, if you are developing an aircraft, that's complex stuff for you and your people to coordinate and deliver on, but what about the sky it must fly in? The weather patterns, thermals, wind, ice, birds, lightning strikes?

No aircraft designer worth their salt would ignore any of those factors, together with a million of others we haven't even thought of.

It may well be worth expanding on KOEs at this point with an example from the UK NHS.

UK NHS is a PPS with more than 1.6 million employees. There is a longstanding and intractable issue whereby accident and emergency (A&E) departments in hospitals have become increasingly overloaded, with ambulances lining up to get to the hospital doors and long waiting times for those who have turned up under their own steam.

Something had to be done. Waiting time targets were introduced immediately to 'encourage' doctors and staff to deal with patients more quickly. That should sort it out, they thought.

Did it sort it out? Of course not - it made matters worse.

Suddenly, A&E staff were watching the clock and devising clever plans to make sure patients didn't breach the magic four-hour limit. Any patient approaching the limit was sent into no-man's land, onto a stretcher or chair in a corridor, or into some other status that kept the statistics in the green. In summary, it drove behaviours opposite to the needs of the patient.

If the people who came up with that solution had been PPS thinkers, they would have taken a completely different approach. They would have traced through the linkages (KOEs) in the system to find out the source of this surge of patients.

It wouldn't have taken long to discover that general practitioners (GPs) over time, and because of changes to contracts, had stopped providing extra hours support, and that patients therefore had a harder time making appointments to see a GP, especially in an emergency.

Chapter Nine

The only surefire way to get emergency treatment was to turn up at A&E where you would not be turned away – even if all you had was a splinter in your finger.

So, we have the solution to the problem, then: GPs' surgeries need to work longer hours.

That would likely be part of it, provided it could be negotiated satisfactorily, but it may not be the complete solution. The entire health and social care PPS would need to be investigated for KOEs to come up with solution(s) to address the root issue(s). Please remember that when we come on to patent law for medical products later; also, keep in mind the saying: 'The love of money is the root of all evil' – another phrase pertinent to our work here.

That leads us nicely onto 'root cause' solutions and our final fundamental for now.

Fundamental No. 5 - Deep rooted solutions to issues in any PPS, (remember, society is a PPS, albeit rather a large one), can only take hold if KOEs allow it to happen.

All this can be wrapped up into a nice little parcel, not necessarily for delivery by our logistics experts above, by paraphrasing Professor Porter in a series of bullet points.

- Value Created (VC) - Cost to Deliver (CD) = Gross Profit (GP).
- VC = What a customer is willing to pay.
- CD = Cost to deliver the value.
- GP increases as VC and CD move in opposite directions, creating ever greater competitive advantage.
- Degree of movement in opposing directions = potential to disrupt.
- Linkages are what create movement in opposite directions.

- KOEs can kill you or make you.
- Keep on doing all this until you become the richest person in the world, à la Mr. Bezos, or those similarly successful as the other exemplars mentioned here.

LEARNING SOMETHING USEFUL FROM THE (MORAL) DWARFS AND DUNCES TOO

Knowing what *not* to do can be as useful as a how-to instruction manual. Let's begin with the UK fixed-term parliament and the Act that created it.

The leadership behind it was that of an uneasy coalition with little concept of the purpose they were trying to accomplish or the possible outcomes they could achieve for themselves – sadly for them and sadly for us too.

When decision-making is conflicted by mixed priorities and power struggles, things can go badly wrong. Without a clear decision-making head on the government's metaphorical shoulders, little attention is given to possible unintended consequences - KOEs in our parlance.

This is the first time we have hit upon the 'people effect', and it is crucial to creating an effective PPS. We all know it, yet pretend it doesn't matter. Aren't we all rational human beings at heart?

So, what should we say about people? Well, you are one, a person that is. That gives you tremendous insight from the start.

You are capable of being greedy, yes? That could mean eating too much chocolate on the weekend or stealing the pennies from a dead man's eyes. Most readers will be in or around the chocolate camp; there will be complete abstainers too, and a small number already dreaming of pockets stuffed to the gunnels with copper.

Chapter Nine

The stark truth is that people, or individuals to be more precise, can screw things up in a PPS. Most times, it happens unintentionally, occasionally on purpose, almost always in pursuit of their own ends. They also have the potential to achieve wonderful things when motivated by a great and powerful good.

As an example of the latter, we turn to an early giant of the pharmaceutical industry, George W. Merck, and his famous words below:

'We try never to forget that medicine is for the people. It is not for the profits. The profits follow, and if we have remembered that, they have never failed to appear. The better we have remembered it, the larger they have been!'

Food for thought, eh?

What is there to take from the insulin example?

In systems thinking theory (ST), the notion of entropy often crops up. It is well known in chemistry and chemical engineering circles as it applies to molecular structures and other scientific workings.

I've tried to get my head around the definitions to be found through search engines and am left scratching my head, feeling deeply inadequate.

The ST definition is much easier to digest. It is basically the tendency for a PPS to fall apart over time if it is not looked after properly. That is, if purpose, outcomes and outputs are not constantly monitored, compared to what's desired, and adjustments made to stay on track, things are likely to turn pear-shaped.

Pear-shaped, of course, is such an inadequate word to describe what has happened with insulin in the US. In fact, there is no word to accurately convey the pain and suffering going on. Look at Twitter and search on *#insulin4all*. The PC PPS is out of control by any measure of human compassion.

Finally, we have Jonas Salk. *'How can you patent the sun?'* he said.

Sadly, and shamefully, there are millions who claim you can. We will prove them wrong, completely and absolutely. Stay with us, it's going to happen.

10 : BROKE'S NO FUN – TIME TO APPLY THE FIX

SORRY, I'M NOT ALLOWED TO TELL YOU THIS

We begin this chapter with a story I'm not allowed to tell you about as I was, and probably still am, bound by confidentiality. Please, therefore, keep what follows under your hat.

It was the one and only time I have been asked to be an expert witness in a litigation; it happened to relate to the US market.

I don't wish to be perceived a braggart, but I must admit the pharmaceutical supply chain is something I know quite a bit about. A lawyer friend of mine in the UK recommended me to his US counterparts as someone competent to carry out the task.

What was the task, did you say?

It was to help prepare a defense to accusations that their client, a very large PC, had colluded with another PC of the generic variety to stitch up the market for a product that had been under patent challenge for some time.

I was provided with all the paperwork on how the supply chain operation had been set up so that those two PCs could work closely together in supplying the market, and that it had been done to the traditional practices expected in this highly regulated industry.

At this point, we need to be careful, and if you don't read this, it's because my editor made me take it out.

Suffice to say that I was asked to stand down after carrying out my analysis and discharged from the job.

THE END OF THE START

This book is the end of our starting activities, to culminate in our conference gathering on 8 May, 2019, when we will gather together in the beautiful Cardiff Bay area to begin a process of righting the wrongs. Techniquest, a home for STEM education in Wales, skilled in catching them young from primary school age, will be our venue.

The attendees will be made up of patients and their representatives, healthcare professionals, pharmacy/other industry professionals, and a panel of specialists, expert in their respective fields. It will be a day for out-of-the-box thinking.

Leading up to the conference, we will level the playing field by providing every attendee with pre-conference educational materials. It will be simple and straightforward. Not quite 'Janet and John', but in that mould. This will ensure that, on the day, we can hit the ground running and no-one is disadvantaged through lack of knowledge.

There will be an output from the day's endeavours, in the form of a white paper which will 'speak truth to power'. There will also be a follow-on book to this one, accessible to anyone who would like to join in.

Let battle commence as we consider again why this must happen.

THE HEARTLESS SYSTEM OF TODAY

If the sad ending to the previous chapter hasn't alerted you to the terrifyingly cruel and heartless state of the medicines system of today, then we should part company now.

If you are still with us, we'll continue with an appeal to those lobbying to maintain the status quo. There will be a lot of

Chapter Ten

opposition from 'the establishment'. I was reminded of this starkly as I submitted my last round of corrections to the manuscript for my previous book, *Find It File It Flog It*. A lady whom I had followed on Twitter messaged me back with a comment on the book preview:

'Good try, but drug companies have too many lobbyists.'

We should therefore begin with a comment aimed at those lobbying to maintain the status quo in this industry:

There are drugs not being developed today because of all the issues and inaction we have discussed at length in the forgoing text. You and your families are not immune to one or more of the conditions that those non-existent treatments could have prevented or cured, no matter how much money you have managed to amass in the course of supporting what we have today. You have a choice therefore: either keep your fingers crossed for you and your loved ones, hoping for the best; or lend a shoulder to the wheel of change that is crying out to turn harder and faster.

If nothing changes in the way the status quo gets to earn its crusts, no amount of cajoling will have any impact. The PPS will go on doing what it's always done. This is where we could use another giant to help us out – enter Professor Russell Ackoff, whom we heard of earlier, with his famous quote: *'Don't fight the system, change the rules and the system will change itself.'*

ANYONE FOR A FIGHT?

This concept from the professor is the cornerstone of what is about to follow. In whatever way we measure the amount of 'broken-ness' in the medicines system of today, there appears to be universal acceptance that the system is not fit for purpose, to phrase it as kindly as possible.

The reaction has been to fight back at the system with increasing intensity as the months and years go by. In the United States especially, politicians of all persuasions are joining the fray. In other parts of the world, where healthcare tends to be funded mainly by the state, there is less frustration and anger, but it is getting there... and rising.

The message from Professor Ackoff is clear: fighting the system while the rules of engagement remain unchanged is a fruitless activity designed to wear us down as each potentially killer lunge and strike is met with a parry and counter-thrust from the opposition.

So, what about this idea of changing the rules?

Cutting to the chase, and hopefully without leading the witness for our conference in May, that is what we will be exploring and, dare we say, recommending. Our full analysis is yet to begin, but we believe there is enough a priori evidence to arrive at a provisional conclusion: changes to patent law as it applies to the medicines industry are required, otherwise, this 'game of thrones' will carry on, unabated, forever and a day.

SIZING UP OUR OPPONENT

There is not too much further to go now before we pack up and get prepared for the pre-conference learning and conference itself.

All that remains is to remind ourselves of the industry PPS as was and as it stands today. Below is where it all started, pre-blockbuster era:

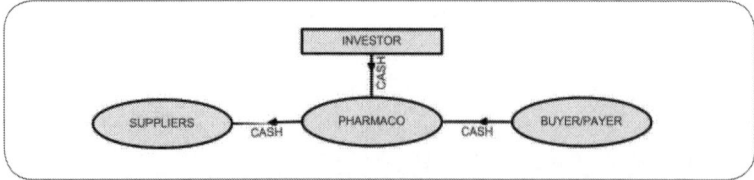

Chapter Ten

Can you believe it was once that simple? A PC would plan to develop and commercialise a new medicine. Investors, realising it could be a bit risky but willing to take a chance, would stump up the funds in the conventional way shareholders do across most industrial sectors.

Nearly all the investors would be pre-existing shareholders in the PC, or banks and other financial institutions offering fair sources of funds to smooth the way.

Armed with the cash, the PC would invest in their people, facilities and supporting infrastructure while sourcing materials and supplies from third parties as necessary.

The ensuing product development programme would be a team effort from people with skin in the game. Products making their way successfully through the commercialisation process would be duly paid for by the hospitals, clinics, physicians' surgeries etc., or via public healthcare funding arrangements.

Then the strategic re-alignment that we learned of in earlier chapters took effect, creating a whole new cadre of players.

Recapping, this is what we have today:

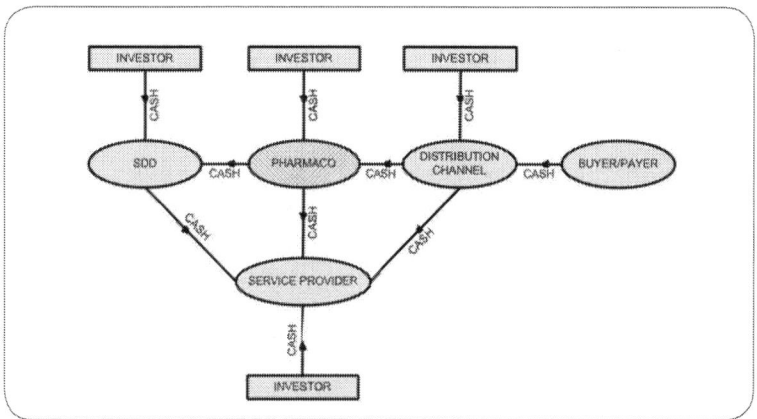

Notice something? (Other than the increase in the number of players in the system...). Rather an explosion in the prevalence of the word 'cash' in there, don't you think? Look too at the BUYER/PAYER - how do the people shelling out the cash for those life-saving medicines get any idea of where their money is going? Good question. I'm blowed if I know.

Anyway, back to the players in the system, with a brief description of them:

PC - A company submitting application(s) for a licence(s) to market medicines for sale. The company could be an innovator (otherwise known as brand or originator) or a generic (copier of innovator products). The company could be dealing in any or all of small molecule (chemically-derived) products, biologic (created as living organisms) products, advanced therapies, such as cell and gene therapies or tissue engineering (also in the biologic product category).

SDD - A company with the intention of developing a medicine up to a certain pre-market stage, selling the intellectual property rights (IPR) it has created on to PCs in return for compensation payments based on key milestones and an agreed share of royalties. Again, an SDD could be operating in any of the product areas listed under PCs above.

SERVICE PROVIDER - A company or individual offering skills and competencies to PCs and SDDs across drug discovery, development and commercialisation, under contract.

These could be:

- Contract manufacturing organisation (CMO)
- Contract development and manufacturing organisation (CDMO)
- Contract research organisation (CRO)
- Third-party logistics provider (3PL)

- An organisation or independent (self-employed) contractor offering services to the industry, such as quality control, testing, and information systems support.

WHOLESALER - A company buying products from PCs with the intention of selling to hospital and community pharmacies, clinics and other end-users of medicines.

PRE-WHOLESALER - Mainly a European concept where storage and logistics services are offered to PCs, under contract. Here, the PC maintains ownership of their products up to the point where they are shipped to buyers. Used in an attempt to circumvent the wholesaler networks, with questionable levels of success.

BUYER/PAYER - A company or individual responsible for paying a WHOLESALER or PRE-WHOLESALER for medicines consumed by end-users. Occasionally, a PC might take payment in special circumstances.

VENTURE CAPITAL (VC) - A venture capitalist is an investor who either provides capital to startup ventures or supports small companies that wish to expand but do not have access to equities markets. Venture capitalists are willing to invest in such companies because they can earn a massive return on their investments if these companies are a success.

PRIVATE EQUITY - Private equity is capital that is not listed on a public exchange. Private equity is composed of funds and investors that directly invest in private companies, or that engage in buyouts of public companies, resulting in the delisting of public equity. Institutional and retail investors provide the capital for private equity, and the capital can be utilised to fund new technology, make acquisitions, expand working capital, and to bolster and solidify a balance sheet.

SHAREHOLDERS - A shareholder is any person, company or other institution that owns at least one share of a company's stock. Because shareholders are a company's owners, they reap the benefits of the company's successes in the form of increased stock valuation. If the company does poorly, however, shareholders can lose money if the price of its stock declines.

This is the landscape we shall be investigating as we move forward to the next stage of analysis – please do stay tuned for further updates.

A WORD FROM PEOPLE WHO CARE

As a final reminder of the battles being fought daily in the word of medicines, let's listen to some of the protagonists, with Ray Perkins to kick off. Ray and I have not met, but we will do at the conference. We met virtually on LinkedIn quite a few years ago and have been having illicit conversations over the internet ever since. He has carried out his work in what would be regarded the orthodox way in non-medicines industries, working hard, focusing on results for end-users of his products, and being a great husband, father and grand-pop. Therefore, he has not made a lot of money, by his own admission.

Take it away, Ray:

Ray C. Perkins, PhD., contrarian. Personal subtitle: 'the mutual seduction of government, pharma and science.'

Engaged in non-dogmatic, non-genomic, integrated drug and diagnostic development.

Relevant publication: *Making the Case for Functional Proteomics*, a manifesto that details systemic failures and provides a rational roadmap to the future.

Chapter Ten

'Both medicine and biology are broken, the pair retrogressing in concert. That brokenness is apparent with a few brief examples. On the medical front, most drugs, old or new, don't work for most people. For a 'good' drug, five sufferers must consume the drug for one sufferer to experience relief. On the 'breakthrough' front, immuno-therapies succeed for only a few percent of the overall disease population. The word 'precise' applies to no treatment, old or new. The lack of precision in medicine is reflected in the lack of precision of decades of biological research.

'Most research efforts cannot be reproduced, including those on which clinical drug trials are based. The failure of reliable research in academic and institutional labs, first noted by industry, dates back over several decades. Many factors contribute to the decline in research, but key among the contributors are an obsessive focus on genomics and the subordination of institutional research to the demands of pharma.

'An effective, efficient and universally beneficial future does not derive from the unreliable past or the broken present. Continuation of the systemic brokenness of medicine and science derives from those who control funding – and those who influence their decisions. Speaking truth to power can be both revolutionary and dangerous, but that truth must be spoken loudly and at every opportunity. "Medicines for the 21st Century" is a stellar opportunity.'

Sit on the fence Ray, why don't you?!

Next up is Becky Middleton with her account, and yes, another virtual LinkedIn-er:

'I am a 43-year-old single female with no children and live alone with my dog in Swindon, Wiltshire. At 24 years of age, I became unwell and received multiple diagnoses. Thirteen years later, a final diagnosis of "Graves disease", a thyroid dysfunction, was made. By this time, I weighed eight stone, had lost much of my hair, suffered chest pains, breathing issues and extreme exhaustion. After failed radiation therapy, I had a total thyroidectomy. Although my health has improved, the medication I use irritates my digestive system which has resulted in polyps having to be removed yearly. At what cost to the NHS?

'The impact of slow diagnosis and poor medical advice has dramatically affected my life. In hindsight, it was a contributing factor to my failed marriage - remaining awake to be in the marriage was a challenge! My self-confidence has taken a hit due to the variations in my weight and a scar which is often mistaken for my being a victim of crime.

'Above all of this, the emotional and financial strain on my family is unmeasurable. Their continued dedication to find a solution for me has cost tens of thousands of pounds, and I am the lucky one.

'My lived experience is the driver behind campaigning for awareness, quicker diagnosis and better maintenance of this illness, along with 38,000 fellow patients who petitioned the government to review, revise and adopt a new diagnosis method.

'It will be my legacy to shape a proposition that will address thyroid disease affecting the lives of 8.2 million known people in the UK.

'Hypo/hyperthyroidism is a medical condition where your autoimmune system attacks the thyroid gland, resulting in your triiodothyronine (T3) or thyroxine (T4) levels to be unbalanced/insufficient. Symptoms can be misdiagnosed as cardiovascular, bipolar, depression, and ME, sometimes resulting in suicide.

'The condition, directly and indirectly, contributes to the nation's low economic productivity; is challenging the National Health Service (NHS); and has a less than adequate research base. My aim is to develop a system that will allow individuals in real-time

Chapter Ten

to manage, monitor, and control their thyroxine levels. I want to permit thousands of men and women, older adults and young people a level of freedom and self-determination which they currently do not have.

'Critically, we need to collate real-time data directly from patients to enable us to truly understand the wider impact and provide evidence to the government and the NHS of the benefits of offering patients full blood, leptin, and diabetes tests and thyroid functions testing. The funding of such study must be impartial and not supported by a drug manufacturer or charity.'

Wow, Becky, such an open, frank and inspirational account, for all the wrong reasons.

'Last, but by no way anywhere near least, is the wonderful and ridiculously endearing Emma Robertson. Emma is the exception to the LinkedIn rule - we met on Facebook. Again, we haven't met face-to-face but will do so for the conference. Judging by her Facebook photos, she likes animals and birds, (pigs, ducks etc) - things that float on water - and disgusting-looking fruit cocktails.

Here are Emma's answers to questions I posed her:

Q: Who are you and what do you do?

A: I am Emma Robertson, a patient activist and campaigner for access to medicines.

I was diagnosed with primary breast cancer in 2013 and received standard 'curative treatment' before being sent away on a drug called Tamoxifen for 5-10 years. In 2015, just one year later, I was diagnosed with secondary breast cancer in my lungs, liver and bones. My oncologist told me this was treatable but not curable. I know where I stand without treatment...

Q: What thoughts do you have on the medicines industry?

A: The medicines industry is a murky, labyrinthine echo-chamber of myth and mystique, with corrupt tendrils wrapped around politicians, charities and public servants. It continues to surprise me how many parties collaborate and collude to ensure such a broken system stays in place.

The loser is, of course, always the patient. We are denied access to medicines that are too expensive, doubt is cast over the efficacy and value of treatments and therapies, and our own research and knowledge is met with scepticism and dismissal.

Q: How do you think this initiative might impact the medicines industry?

A: My hope is that this initiative will give me some explosive ammunition to take back to my colleagues and friends who feel they have no alternative but to continue to collude. Even when the rails have been dug from beneath the train, without an alternative route, it seems that train is only able to continue on its tried and tested pathway. I would like to take home some viable new directions of travel!

We will do that with you Emma – our pleasure.

Chapter Ten

CLOSING REMARKS

Having been careful not to assign blame to individuals going about their business in PPSs around the world, there must be one overriding caveat applied: those at the top of the tree can't throw their arms in the air and claim it was the system wot done it. They are responsible for making it what it is today.

When pharma CEOs part company with their employers, with payouts ranging from the hundreds of thousands to $610M, it should not have escaped their attention how little they delivered to the lives of patients and how much damage they inflicted along the way.

We rest our case, for now.

APPENDICE 1 : EDUCATION PROGRAMME AND WORKSHOP

Medicines Development - The Fundamentals

Presenter: Hedley Rees, managing consultant, PharmaFlow Ltd., author *Supply Chain Management In The Drug Industry*, J Wiley, NJ, 2011.

Aim:

The course aims to equip attendees with foundational knowledge in preparation for an interactive workshop be held 8th May, 2019, at Techniquest, Cardiff Bay. The title of the workshop is 'Medicines for the 21St Century: Safe, Better, Cheaper', and the output will be a white paper to be presented to key stakeholders in the medicines industry, including parliamentary cross-party committees.

Delegate Profile:

Delegates will be curated from patients, patient groups, primary and secondary healthcare professionals, and industry professionals such as pharmacists. Also on-hand will be a facilitation panel of expert specialists available to share their knowledge on the day (below); they will also undertake the course so that a single baseline is set for the day. Total attendance will be c. 300.

Learning objectives:

- Understand how healthcare and medicines systems engage and interact
- Gain an appreciation of the stages of medicines R&D and the medicines approval process

- Investigate areas where patients could gainfully contribute
- Step through the stages in the medicines supply chain
- Explore current issues and opportunities relating to safety, efficacy and affordability of medicines.

Overview of course structure

- Invitations: 4th March – 28th March.
- Distribute materials: 29th March.
- Read materials: 1st April – 3rd May.
- Companion book available for purchase w/c 29th April (optional).
- Interactive workshop: 8th May 2019 at Techniquest, Cardiff Bay.
- Post-workshop: Review of outputs and construction of white paper.

Guiding principles for the workshop

- Dialogue rather than discussion: Listen, reflect, respond, repeat.
- Collaborate and learn: Engage with others, reach out, support.
- Ask questions: No such thing as a stupid question.
- Chip-in with ideas: Out-of-the-box is perfectly OK.
- Disseminate learning to others: Tell others about what you've learned.
- Become a FOMM: Friend of Medicines Modernisation

Appendice One

Workshop day

There will be three themes:
- Safe medicines
- Better medicines
- Cheaper medicines

The team at Techniquest is expert in facilitating interactive workshops for school children – they will be applying those skills to design the day. Adults are likely to be more of a challenge, but they seem confident they can nail it!

Our aim will be to maximise exchange of knowledge and information. Full details will be provided with the pre-conference documentation.

PRE-CONFERENCE SUBJECT MATTER

The pre-conference reading will be made up of five modules:
- People-Purpose Systems (PPS)
- Medicines R&D
- Improving Patient Involvement in the medicines life-cycle
- Medicines Supply Chain
- Issues and Opportunities in 20th Century Medicines

APPENDICE 2 : MEDICINES FOR THE 21ST CENTURY - FACILITATION PANEL MEMBERS

Dr. GARY ACTON, Cancer Clinician at Pirates of Oncology; Senior Medical Advisor at Cancer Research-UK; Author of *Sympathy for the Devil*, a bestselling book on the biotech industry.

Specialist area(s) for the conference: oncology; clinical drug development; and biotech industry.

Dr. LIZ BREEN, Reader in Health Service Operations at University of Bradford School of Pharmacy and Medical Sciences, Bradford, UK.

Specialist area(s) for the conference: sustainability practices in pharmacy; reverse logistics; process mapping in healthcare; and medicines optimisation.

JIM CAMBELL, PhD, Founder/Former CEO/Consultant of SureScreen Scientifics; Director of Morley Life Sciences Ltd.

Specialist area(s) for the conference: precision medicine; diagnostics; and scouring the world for new therapies.

PROFESSOR RENA CONTI, Associate Professor of Markets, Public Policy, and Law at Questrom School of Business, Boston University, Boston.

Specialist area(s) for the conference: US Health System Innovation and Policy; drug wars in the US.

ABIGAIL COOPER, Civil Aerospace Quality Manager at Rolls-Royce, Derby, UK.

Specialist area(s) for the conference: quality management systems; civil aviation; and improvement & change management.

MARK DUMAN, Catalyst, Consultant, Connector, Patient, (and Advocate)

Specialist area(s) for the conference: patient perspectives, and medicines-taking and pharmacy.

PROFESSOR GRAHAM DUTFIELD, Professor of International Governance at the University of Leeds.

Specialist area(s) for the conference: intellectual property; health; genetics; and biotechnology.

Dr. PETER FELDSCHREIBER, Barrister at Chambers of Sue Carr QC, London, UK

Specialist area(s) for the conference: medical and healthcare law; pharmaceutical and medical devices regulatory law; and life with dual qualifications as a barrister and physician.

CATHERINE GEYMAN, Director & Risk Management Consultant, Intersys Ltd., UK

Specialist area(s) for the conference: Pharma supply chain, and risk modelling & management.

ALAN KENNEDY, Executive Director of Pharma TEAM-UP and Team Poseidon Ltd. London, UK.

Specialist area(s) for the conference: collaboration methods; Pharma logistics; and tireless working to establish a presence in the industry.

Appendice Two

PROFESSOR MINESH KHASHU, Consultant Neonatologist & Prof. of Perinatal Health with NHS & Bournemouth University

Specialist area(s) for the conference: the NHS; Collaboration; and healthcare management and leadership.

PROFESSOR VANYA LOROCH, Educator in life sciences and biotechnology at Loroch CTLS; Professor at Lausanne Business School; and Education Director of Swiss Biotech.

Specialist area(s) for the conference: precision medicine; biotech and science storytelling; communication and training.

DR. ERIC LOW, Eric Low Consulting; Member, Board of Directors of Myeloma Canada; Member, Board of Trustees of the David Forbes-Nixon Foundation.

Specialist area(s) for the conference: clinical research; myeloma; and patient advocacy.

EDWARD NARKE, PhD, Principal & Regulatory Managing Director of Design Space Inpharmatics LLC, Greater Philadelphia.

Specialist area(s) for the conference: Quality by Design (QbD), and Regulatory Chemistry, Manufacturing & Controls (CMC).

PROFESSOR ANANT PARADKAR, Professor of Pharmaceutical Engineering Science at the Centre for Pharmaceutical Engineering Science, University of Bradford.

Specialist area(s) for the conference: process and product innovation; process understanding; and transdermal drug delivery.

ZACK PEMBERTON-WHITELEY, Patient Advocacy Director at Leukaemia Care, and Chair of the Acute Leukaemia Advocates Network.

Specialist area(s) for the conference: leukaemia; patient advocacy; health technology appraisals; patient surveys; and campaigns.

RAY PERKINS, PhD, President & CEO of New Liberty Proteomics Corp., New Liberty, KY.

Specialist area(s) for the conference: drug discovery; protein chemistry; and biotechnology.

EUR ING KEITH PLUMB, Owner & Director of Integra Pharma Services Ltd., and Trustee of IChemE, UK.

Specialist area(s) for the conference: process, equipment, and safety consultant, and facility design.

PROFESSOR DIPAK RAMJI, Professor of Cardiovascular Science at Cardiff University.

Specialist area(s) for the conference: cardiovascular disease; drug discovery; natural products; inflammation; molecular biology; and immunology.

HEDLEY REES, Author and Managing Consultant at Pharmaflow Ltd., Bridgend, UK.

Specialist area(s) for the conference: new model for medicines development; and operations & supply chain management.

PROFESSOR PARAG SINGHAL, Consultant Endocrinologist with Bristol NHS; Hon. National Secretary of the British Association of Physicians of Indian Origin (BAPIO), UK.

Specialist area(s) for the conference: endocrinology, and NHS improvement & efficient utilisation of resources.

PROFESSOR KESHAV SINGHAL, MBE, Consultant Orthopaedic Surgeon at the Princess of Wales Hospital, Bridgend; and Chair of BAPIO, Wales, UK.

Specialist area(s) for the conference: innovation in the NHS; healthcare management; and government policy.

Appendice Two

PROFESSOR JUSTIN STEBBING, Professor of Cancer Medicine and Oncology at Imperial College, London, and Editor-in-Chief at Oncogene, London.

Specialist area(s) for the conference: oncology; editing, clinical practice; and medicine.

PROFESSOR DANIEL STEENSTRA, Royal Academy of Engineering Visiting Professor in Medical Innovation at Cranfield University, Bedford, UK.

Specialist area(s) for the conference: medical & disruptive innovation, and product design.

JESÚS ZURDO, PhD, SVP - Process Science & Innovation at Rentschler Biopharma, Laupheim, Germany

Specialist area(s) for the conference: development & manufacture of therapeutic biopharmaceuticals; biochemistry; and molecular biology.

ADVISORS

PROFESSOR ANDREW COX, President Emeritus at IIAPS (International Institute for Advanced Purchasing and Supply).

Specialist area(s) for the conference: strategic procurement, and supply sourcing, category management, power and dependence in supply chains.

PATRICK CROWLEY PhD, Founder & Owner of Callum Consultancy; and Former VP of Pharmaceutical Development at GlaxcoSmithKline-US, (37 years at GSK).

Specialist area(s) for the conference: dosage form development and evaluation.

PROFESSOR DONALD INGBER, Director of the Wyss Institute for Biologically Inspired Engineering, Harvard University, Boston, USA.

Specialist area(s) for the conference: biologically-inspired engineering; cell biology; and medical engineering.

CLIVE MEANWELL, MD, PhD, Chief Innovation Officer & Founder and CEO, 2004 - 2018 of The Medicines Company.

Specialist area(s) for the conference: medical innovation; the US healthcare system; and playing rugby for London Irish in the 1980s.

TONY WEIR, NED, Entrepreneur, former CFO and COO in the biotech and healthcare sectors.

Specialist area(s) for the conference: listed company finance and accounting, acquisitions, life science, and healthcare operations.

References

1. *(Pg 31)* Gaynes R. The Discovery of Penicillin—New Insights After More Than 75 Years of Clinical Use. Emerg Infect Dis. 2017;23(5):849-853. https://wwwnc.cdc.gov/eid/article/23/5/16-1556_article

2. *(Pg 44)* http://cen.acs.org/articles/92/web/2014/11/Tufts-Study-Finds-Big-Rise.html

3. *(Pg 67)* Checkland, Peter, Systems Thinking, Systems Practice, J Wiley & Sons, 1999